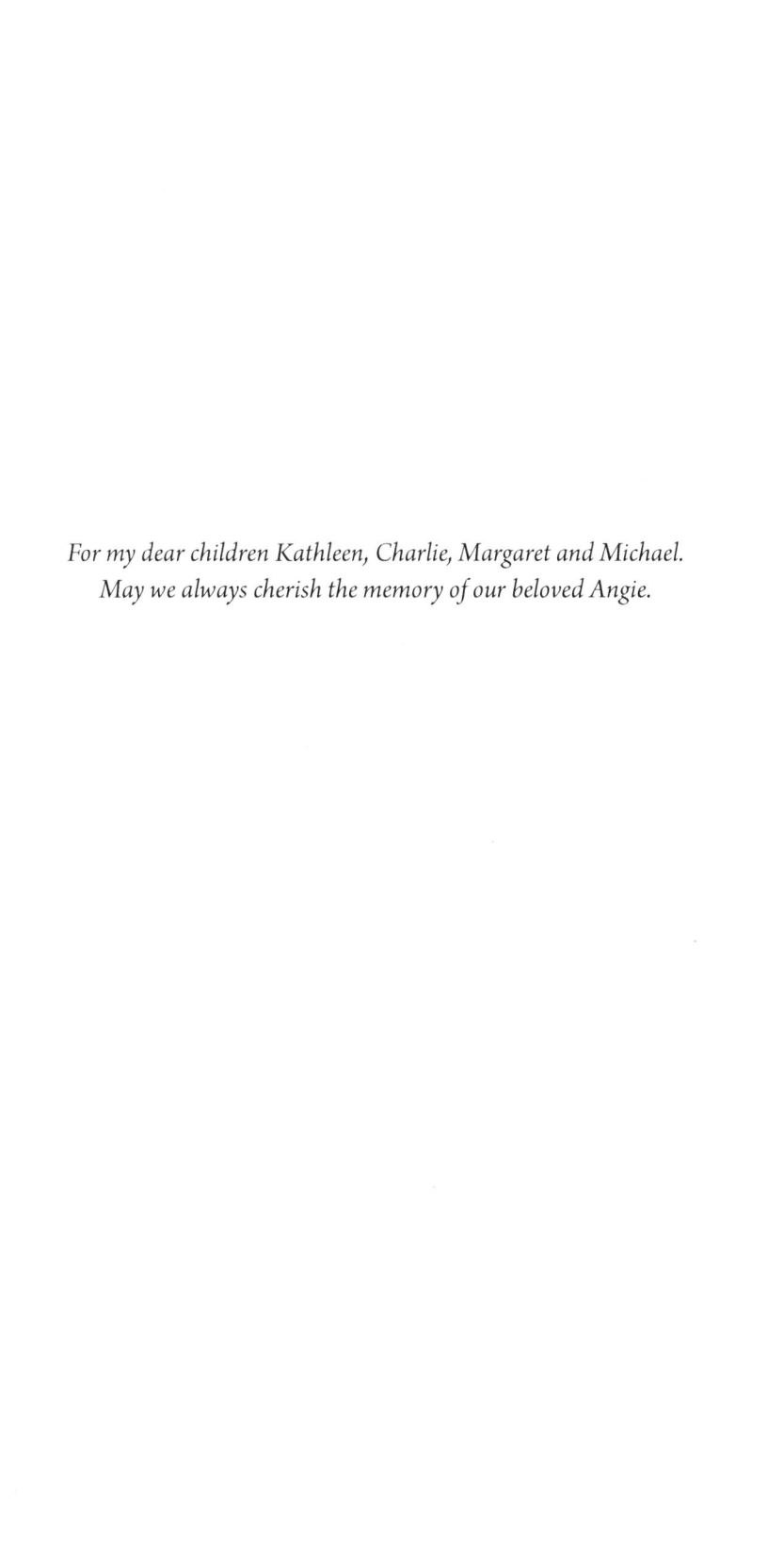

*For my dear children Kathleen, Charlie, Margaret and Michael.
May we always cherish the memory of our beloved Angie.*

CONTENTS

Introduction 7
Chapter 1:   Beginnings of a Beautiful Life 9
Chapter 2:   Tying the Knot and Living the Dream 14
Chapter 3:   Making Her Mark 26
Chapter 4:   From Newlyweds to Partners 35
Chapter 5:   Raising Our Legacy 49
Chapter 6:   Miles of Memories 77
Chapter 7:   Thirty-three Years of Us 95
Chapter 8:   Braving the Darkness 107
Chapter 9:   A Light That Never Fades 121
Chapter 10: Memories Shared, Lives Touched 138
Chapter 11: Why Angie Matters 152
Acknowledgements 157
About the Author 159

INTRODUCTION

At six-thirty on a chilly November morning in 2024, I am awakened by the sound of my two little barking dogs (a shih tzu and Pekingese). I slowly pivot my seventy-three-year-old body from the king-size bed and place my feet on the cool floor, disappointed that the rare October heat wave has dissipated and the morning temperature hovers around freezing. Winter is near. Golf must wait until spring. I busy myself with the usual rituals of drinking strong coffee, skimming the digital *New York Times* on my iPad, scrolling through apps on my smartphone, and thinking about what to do today.

This has been my postretirement routine for the past seven years after a tragic turn in life when my wife of thirty-three years, Angie, a beautiful red-haired Irish lass from Chicago's South Side, passed away peacefully after a four-year entanglement with the fatal brain cancer, glioblastoma. Simply put, Angie was a bright and shining star. She was the love of my life, a beautiful woman, a devoted partner, and the mother of our four children. She truly was a blessing and her death was a brutal loss, bringing on years of sorrow and loneliness. Memories of life with Angie are joyful yet sad. I think about our life together every day and photos of us are displayed prominently around our large lake house, which she designed.

Angie never felt sorry for herself or thought the cards were stacked against her. When she encountered obstacles, she summoned her strong will to succeed and more often than not, she beat the odds. I hope her story can bring smiles, arouse warm feelings, and most importantly, inspire those who might feel overwhelmed by life's obstacles to learn helpful lessons from Angie's life.

I'm retired from a five-decade career in public relations. I worked for organizations in government and politics, the pharmaceutical industry, and as a self-employed consultant. I was fortunate to achieve professional and financial success in business and be able to support—with strong help from Angie—our four children. In retirement, I now teach advertising and public relations courses at the University of Wisconsin-Whitewater. I enjoy sharing my expertise and experiences with students and also appreciate what they teach me.

I'm blessed with a loving family that now includes seven grandchildren. They bring great joy to my life, even though I mourn that Angie isn't with us to enjoy and nurture the grandkids. I often think about how much she would love them and get involved in their lives with their moms and dads—our daughters, Kathleen and Margaret; daughters-in-law, Kelsey and Maura; sons, Charlie and Michael; and sons-in-law, Paul and Matt.

I'm writing this memoir for bereavement purposes and as my overdue tribute to Angie. Her life story is about confronting obstacles to achieving one's life goals and doing what it takes to overcome them. The grandchildren were a source of inspiration for my writing. I believe they should learn the story of their grandmother's life and know how her legacy will influence their lives.

Rather than telling the story from beginning to end, I have organized the book into various topics, such as career, travel and child-rearing. What follows are chapters covering the beginning and early years of my relationship with Angie, highlights of our thirty-three years of married life, and stories from the four years we spent coping with the diagnosis of a fatal cancer. In the last chapter, I write about what I believe is Angie's legacy and how her story can provide encouragement and inspiration for those trying to overcome life's obstacles.

Chapter 1

BEGINNINGS OF A BEAUTIFUL LIFE

It was 1980. I was twenty-nine and living in a small Georgian-style home in Westchester, Illinois, which I bought from my younger brother, Tom, following his divorce and job transfer to Minneapolis. The house was five blocks west of my parents' Georgian where I was raised. I was two years old when they bought the place my dad called his starter home. Little did he know then that it would be the only home he would ever own.

I was working as press secretary for the Illinois state treasurer, a wealthy trucking company owner with strong political connections he leveraged with campaign donations to acquire support for his bid to be the first Italian American elected to statewide office in Illinois. I met him by chance in 1977 when a political acquaintance introduced us at a cocktail lounge called Key West in Countryside, Illinois. The place had no resemblance to the paradise at the southern tip of Florida. The three of us talked for two hours as the trucker explained his intention to run for state treasurer. He said he had the backing of the powerful Cook County Regular Democratic Organization. The nomination to be the Democratic Party's candidate was a cinch, he claimed, and I believed him.

The prospective candidate liked me because my political ally told him he needed a smart well-spoken campaign aide who knew how to deal with the news media. He was impressed that I had a master's degree in political science and was teaching part time at Mundelein College, an all-female school on the far north side of the city on Lake Michigan. It's now part of Loyola University. My role would be to get positive media coverage for the campaign, which could help prevent massive losses expected in heavily Republican suburban and downstate counties. Looking back, I'm sure favorable media coverage of the campaign was a contributing factor in winning the election.

The victory netted me the press secretary's job and a yearly salary of $19,000, the most money I ever made. I developed strong contacts with political reporters which helped my boss stay in the news. My job was fun. I ran in Chicago's fast-moving political scene, making influential friends who were good for lots of favors.

In 1982, my boss ran for the office of Illinois secretary of state and trailed badly throughout the campaign. When you are behind in the polls, it can be tough to raise money, so our campaign couldn't buy enough television ads to be competitive. We lost the election, and I needed a new job.

A year earlier in October 1981, I met a good friend, Bill, from the campaign and his girlfriend, Marion, at a favorite bar on Chicago's trendy Rush Street, Butch McGuire's. Over several drinks, we talked about the upcoming election and the likelihood that my boss would lose and maybe lose big. They did their best to console me about the expected loss. Marion asked if I was seeing anyone romantically. The answer was no and, truthfully, I had not been in a serious love relationship since graduating from college in 1973. There were short-term flings and one-night stands over the last nine years with ladies in Chicago and Springfield, the state capital. But no relationship lasted more than a few months. A few had potential to advance to serious relationships but fell short. Feelings on my end simply weren't strong enough.

Marion wanted to introduce me to her best friend, Angie. I agreed and Marion offered to arrange a double date at a popular Italian eatery, Palermo's in Oak Lawn, best known for its fettuccine alfredo. I was the last to arrive on that chilly October Friday night due to heavy traffic from downtown Chicago, where I worked for the state at the time. I hung my Bogart-style trench coat in the unattended coatroom and walked past the bar to look for my friends. I found them seated in a booth at the back of the dining room. There was a colorful mural of Venice canals on the back wall. Bill and Marion were parked together and Angie was sitting alone across from them.

Before sitting down, I stopped about ten feet from the booth and stared at Angie. She sat with perfect posture and I focused on her lovely Irish features—red hair, light skin, and an engaging smile. Instantly, I was attracted to her. Her demeanor was friendly and reserved. I greeted Angie with a "Nice to meet you" handshake and sat. The threesome already had ordered drinks: a beer for Bill and white wine for Angie and Marion. I ordered Dewar's White Label Scotch on the rocks.

Conversation throughout the evening was mostly small talk about our jobs, families, and the campaign, although Bill and I chatted a lot with a friend at a nearby table. But Angie hardly spoke. I asked her a few boring questions trying to initiate conversation and convince her to like me. I was attracted to her style with her permed shoulder length red hair and a crisply pressed white-cotton blouse. Snug blue jeans and stylish boots completed her outfit. My efforts at conversation didn't go well. Angie had mastered the art of one- or two-word answers while conveying her annoyance.

After we finished our entrées—chicken for the ladies and pasta for Bill and me—we decided to call it a night and said our goodbyes. I looked at Angie and said I enjoyed being with her. She said, "Thank you," and I asked for her phone number, which she wrote on a cocktail napkin. After the glowing buildup from Marion, my expectations were hopeful. Maybe this could be the one woman I could fall in love with after so long. But I didn't feel she was the least bit interested in me, so I chose not to pursue further contact and tossed her phone number. It was just another disappointing date.

After a couple of weeks, I learned from Marion that Angie hadn't been feeling well the night of our double date. She had wanted to cancel, but Marion insisted she show up. Well, maybe that explained the cold shoulder treatment, but it wasn't enough to prompt me to try my luck again with her. I told Marion I wasn't going to call Angie.

A year later, in the summer of 1982, I was playing golf, teaching part time at Mundelein, and umpiring baseball and softball games—all while still working for the state and the reelection campaign. I was making enough dough to pay green fees, bar tabs and the mortgage on the Westchester Georgian. On a hot Saturday in early August, Marion hosted a thirtieth birthday celebration for Bill at her parents' home in Evergreen Park, just south of Chicago. Marion's father was the boss at a popular dinner-theater restaurant called the Martinique. So the food served at the party was outstanding with plentiful pizza, salad, and pasta.

I arrived after playing 18 holes at a nearby club. While helping myself to a cold beer from the Miller Lite keg, I turned and was face-to-face with Angie who was next in line. It was an awkward moment. I hadn't seen her since the failed double date at Palermo's. I tried to be cool, poured her a beer, and gestured for us to step away from the keg. We talked. She was very attractive, as usual, and our conversation surprisingly was warm and friendly. After fifteen minutes, she excused herself to chat with some girlfriends. Before she left, I asked if she would have dinner with me the following weekend. She answered yes. I said I would call her in a few days, but since I had tossed her phone number at Palermo's, I had to ask Marion for it. "You had better call her this time," warned Marion.

The story of my first official date with Angie could have been written for a low-budget romance movie. I picked up Angie at her bungalow apartment in Chicago's Marquette Park neighborhood. Before we left, I met her older sister and roommate Mimi, a cardiac nurse at the now closed Michael Reese Hospital. She was friendly but probably wondered why Angie was going out with me. We had a 7:30 p.m. reservation at an upscale seafood restaurant, the Chestnut Street Grill, in the eight-story Water Tower Place shopping structure on Michigan Avenue. The restaurant was on the second floor.

On the way to dinner, Angie and I talked about our friends and families and some favorite television shows. In Chicago, it was Venetian Night on the lakefront, which was a late-August tradition. Boats decorated with bright Italian lights cruised the shoreline and we watched them go by from the car. I was carefully keeping my eyes on the road while navigating traffic on Lake Shore Drive. Once seated at the restaurant, I asked if we should order a bottle of wine. Angie said she'd like that. The waiter recommended an expensive chardonnay, which I ordered to impress my date. It was cold, crisp, and buttery with a nice finish—a perfect pairing with our swordfish entrées. We talked happily and decided to head back to Angie's apartment after dinner instead of staying for a nightcap.

The drive back was chatty and the Venetian Night festivities had concluded. I walked Angie to her front door and wondered if I should kiss her good night. All the vibes were positive. So I placed my right arm around her shoulders and planted a tender smooch. What happened next was a scene from the movies. As our lips parted, Angie's eyes fluttered, and she collapsed against me and slumped to the doorway floor. She fainted on the door step. I felt like Cary Grant and guided her to a nearby couch. She recovered fast and said she couldn't believe what happened. I couldn't believe it either. I hugged her and we kissed again. Asked if feeling okay, she nodded yes, and I bade her good night and said I would call in a few days. Driving home, I kept thinking about the fainting incident. I was thrilled with our time together. It was the first date I had had in years that made me excited about a future relationship, if I played my cards right. I knew I would soon fall in love.

Chapter 2

TYING THE KNOT AND LIVING THE DREAM

During the next few months and through the holidays, the pace of our relationship exceeded the speed limit, and our feelings for each other easily moved from affection to love. Angie and I usually got together twice a week, with me staying overnight at her place. We saw movies, went to bars to meet friends, and dined at favorite restaurants in her neighborhood or downtown. One memorable time was a birthday party for her oldest brother John, a Chicago fireman. On that night, I met Angie's brothers and sisters and her parents, who were Irish immigrants, and many of the family's friends. The party was loud with lots of country music, laughter, and beer. It seemed that everyone wanted to meet Angie's new boyfriend. I felt like the guest of honor even though it wasn't my birthday. I had a lot of fun at the party, and so did Angie. It was the beginning of many lifelong friendships.

With each date, Angie and I grew closer. I was hooked. I fell in love with her fast and hoped someday she would be my wife. I was enchanted by her gorgeous smile, sweet personality, and fun sense of humor. In the first year of our dating relationship, we frequently stayed overnight at our places and enjoyed the Chicago social scene at nice restaurants, trendy bars, sporting events (Cubs and Bulls), theaters, and museums. One night we had dinner at my favorite Italian restaurant, the Como

Inn, and went to the Bulls game after dinner. We had tickets to watch the Bulls play the Atlanta Hawks and their star rookie, Dominique Wilkins—known as the Human Highlight Reel for his acrobatic dunks. The Bulls won the game, but what I remember most is when I presented the tickets to the usher he said, "Sit wherever you want." That was a year before Michael Jordan arrived and the franchise began a long run of consecutive sell-outs. There were only five thousand fans in attendance that night. Angie had never been to a Bulls game.

One summer weekend in 1983, Angie and I decided to sneak away for a couple of days in Lake Geneva, Wisconsin, which is the most popular weekend getaway for Illinois folks (known as flatlanders by Wisconsin natives, whom Illinois people call cheeseheads). We drove to Lake Geneva on Saturday and checked into the Geneva Lake Inn, a decent, inexpensive motel with a swimming pool. We bought a bottle of chardonnay and finished it poolside. Late in the afternoon, we went back to the room, napped for a couple of hours, showered, and dressed to go out for dinner. Ralph's Steakhouse near downtown Lake Geneva was our chosen dining spot. We picked it from a brochure in the motel lobby. At the bar before sitting down for dinner, I ordered a bourbon Manhattan straight up, and to my surprise, white-wine drinker Angie ordered one too. She asked me if she would like the drink. I assured her that she would. We enjoyed our first Manhattan, and our second, and our third. By then we thought it was a good idea to soak up the booze with a thick juicy steak. Those were the first and last Manhattans Angie drank in my thirty-five years with her.

There is a banker's box in a basement closet that holds thirty or more funny, cute, and loving cards Angie sent me before we were married. Every time one appeared in the mailbox I grinned at this gesture of love. Some of the cards had suggestive messages like "Want to fool around?" while others simply had clever and humorous ways to say I love you. On the day Angie died, I couldn't resist the urge to find that box and look at the cards. Just seeing her handwriting aroused deep feelings and wonderful memories. I smiled and cried. After about an hour, I put the box back in the closet and haven't opened it since.

The year 1983 was very good for me. In April, I was hired for a public relations position at Abbott Laboratories. My title was media relations specialist and the pay was $35,000 a year, by far my personal high. I thought getting hired at Abbott was a long shot because I had no corporate or PR agency experience and knew nothing about Abbott or its businesses and markets. Fortunately, a manager in the human relations department liked my résumé and was impressed with my politics and government experience working with the news media. The first interview with the HR manager was basically a screening test to see if I was qualified enough to warrant moving on to interviews in the public affairs department.

On the night before the Abbott interview, Angie and I talked for an hour on the phone. I told her about the job and rehearsed some answers I would give to expected questions. She could tell I wasn't sure about how I would perform. "This job is perfect for you," she said. "Just be yourself and show them how smart you are." I appreciated the confidence boost.

As the first interview at Abbott progressed, I wasn't sure how I was doing. Despite the encouragement from Angie, I was nervous. That changed when I was asked about my biggest challenge in public relations. I perked up and beamed with confidence. I thought if I couldn't knock this one out of the park, I didn't deserve to be hired. I proceeded to explain my role in handling the Chicago media—which included on-camera TV interviews—following the gruesome murder of the longtime chief financial officer for the state treasurer's office. He was found in a Michigan Avenue hotel room naked, tied to the bed by his wrists and ankles, and gagged with a handkerchief. My boss and I had to identify the body. It was an experience I certainly won't forget. I had never seen a murder victim before and haven't seen one since. It turned out our very conservative and soft-spoken bean counter led a kinky gay double life for years when he came from Springfield to Chicago for regular meetings with public funds officers at the LaSalle Street banks that held millions in deposits of state funds.

The interviews in the PR department were encouraging, and I hadn't given any wrong answers that might kill my chances to get the job. The facial expressions of the two interviewers (who would be my future colleagues) were friendly and supportive. The last interview that day put me in front of the vice president of public affairs. He was in his mid-forties, very formal, and sat ramrod straight behind a huge desk in his expensive dark blue suit, white shirt, and red tie—the classic IBM corporate look. I expected a tough interview. But the VP asked a few perfunctory questions about my résumé and told me he received positive feedback from my previous interviewers. Next, he shocked me by saying congratulations. I got the job! Driving home from Abbott I couldn't help but think about the first interview and my answer describing that awful murder. The story got me past the screening interview and on to the PR department. Without it, I might have been sent home. Recounting a terrible crime is what led to the beginning of my corporate public relations career.

Angie was thrilled when I called to tell her the news of my hiring. She said she knew I would get the job. I recapped the interviews for her, including the story about the murdered state official, which I had never told her. "You saw a naked guy who was strangled? What was that like?" she asked.

After learning I was hired at Abbott, maybe lurking in the back of her mind was a thought that I could afford an engagement ring. We immediately planned a celebration dinner at, of all places, Palermo's. My next call was to Mom who said she was very proud of me and wished me good luck in my new job.

I was supposed to start at Abbott in two weeks. My first task was to buy a couple of business suits to help me fit in properly in the corporate environment. I went to Marshall Field's department store in Oakbrook. Field's was the premier high-end retailer in the Chicago market with flagship stores on State Street in Chicago's Loop, in Water Tower Place, and several in suburban shopping malls. My mother was a dedicated Field's shopper and was pleased I was going to buy my suits there. I tried on several and settled on two Botany 500 single-breasted suits, one navy blue and the other a gray pinstripe. They would be tailored and ready for me to look sharp in a week.

As summer turned into fall in 1983, I no longer could wait to pop the question and propose to Angie. I was now thirty-two and had finally done it. I had fallen in love with the superstar lady of my dreams and worked up the courage to ask her to be my wife for life. So as we sat on her couch after returning from a favorite Mexican restaurant and cuddled, I took the leap. My stomach was churning in anticipation, and it wasn't from the Mexican food. I was nervous. What if she said no? How would I respond? There was no dramatic on-my-knees "Will you marry me" plea. I played it straight.

Turning to Angie, I said, "I love you very much, so will you marry me?" I realized I was being too businesslike, and I didn't think Angie was surprised by my question. But her eyes moistened. She said *"Yes."* We hugged and kissed passionately.

I was overcome with relief when she said yes. My practical German side didn't want to buy an engagement ring until I knew Angie wanted to marry me. Why buy an expensive gift you might have to return? We decided to go ring shopping the following weekend.

A travel agent I knew worked in the Mallers Building at 5 South Wabash in downtown Chicago, which is home to numerous wholesale jewelry businesses. It was known by some as a den of thieves. Floor after floor was full of jewelry vendors. My travel agent friend recommended one who he said was honest and would give us a good deal on a nice ring. We made an appointment to meet with the jeweler and found him, as advertised, to be seemingly honest and very accommodating. He showed Angie several different ring styles at various prices. I was just an observer knowing my opinion wouldn't be worth much. She decided on a modest quarter carat diamond in a gold-band setting with diamond chips around the ring. It was a great choice. Angie was very happy with it. The ring was ready in a week, just in time for the holidays.

Newly engaged, we spent our second Christmas together in 1983, and we spent Christmas Eve at Angie's parents' house. Angie's brothers and sisters were there and so were some of her fireman brother's friends. Folks were singing Christmas carols and downing beer and whiskey. When I rang the front doorbell, Angie's burly Irish father answered. I greeted him with a bottle of Black Bush Irish Whiskey. He said, "Let's hide this, I don't want those guys to see it." What he meant is he didn't want me to show up with the bottle and encourage the guys to drink more. He thought they'd had enough. And he was right.

The highlight of the evening, and something that was talked about for many years afterward, was our singing of "O Holy Night." As we moved through the lyrics, we sang the line "Fall on your knees" and at that moment Angie's mother, Hannah, fell to her knees. It was spontaneous and hilarious. The laughter probably was heard throughout the neighborhood. The fall-on-your-knees moment was recalled fondly for many years in the family.

After the impromptu party, Angie and I spent the rest of the evening at her apartment, drank wine, and exchanged gifts. We agreed to go easy on Christmas gifts due to the anticipated wedding costs, for which we would be paying. I gave her a Mikimoto pearl necklace (I didn't go easy; couldn't resist), and she gave me a stylish warm winter coat.

Wedding planning dominated the first nine months of 1984. The big day was set for September 15, 1984. The ceremony was to be held at Angie's home parish church, St. Bede the Venerable, and the reception would be at the Martinique restaurant, where Angie worked as the administrative assistant to the owner. It was the premier wedding venue on the South Side. We decided to honeymoon for ten days—three in San Francisco and seven in Maui. We included time in San Francisco because I had visited the city a few times and wanted to share its charms with my new bride.

Our wedding day was a beautiful sunny fall afternoon and my day started at 8:00 a.m. with a trip to the tuxedo-rental store to pick up my suit. The black tux coat had tails, which I thought was cool. Angie's day started at her parents' house with a make-up session for her and the bridesmaids. I got dressed alone in my home and thought about keeping my cool and nerves in check during the wedding ceremony. It didn't happen, as I sweated profusely on the altar.

Our priest was a friend whom I knew from the election campaign. He was the editor of an Italian fraternal newsletter and director of an Italian American nursing home called Villa Scalabrini. He was a celebrity in the Italian American community. I was very pleased he was able to preside at our wedding. My favorite memory of my now deceased friend is when he invited my mother and me to attend Mass at the Villa on Thanksgiving. Cardinal Joseph Bernadin was to preside, and my friend knew my mother attended Mass every day and would be thrilled to meet the cardinal. I was so grateful he thought about us and extended the invite. It still is a very fond memory.

Early in the afternoon, I picked up Mom and we rode together to St. Bede's. My dad was disabled from a stroke, and Mom decided he shouldn't be at the wedding and reception. I think she wanted to have a good time and knew that wasn't possible if she had to mind Dad. It wasn't selfish, because she had to take care of Dad every day and was entitled for one day to have a break and enjoy the wedding. I had mixed feelings about her decision but didn't object. I was going to suggest having his nurse be on hand but knew she would reject that idea.

The wedding ceremony featured a young girl singer who was related to a friend of Angie's. She had a magnificent voice and everyone in the church was wowed by her rendition of "Ave Maria" at the end of the ceremony. To say the bride was exceptionally beautiful would be a major understatement. She was gorgeous almost beyond belief. As Angie walked down the aisle arm in arm with her father, I couldn't stop looking at her. I kept thinking, *This goddess is about to become my wife.* After we exchanged vows and rings, Angie did the traditional walk to the statue of the Blessed Virgin Mary, placed a rose at the foot of the statue, knelt for a short prayer, and returned to the altar next to me. We held hands on the altar. This occurred while the singer enchanted everyone with her "Ave Maria." After that, we turned to the crowd and raised our tightly held hands above our heads to the sound of joyous applause.

In the time between pictures and the wedding reception, I asked the limo driver to take us on the half-hour drive to my parents' home in Westchester. We surprised my dad and his nurse looking like models in our splendid wedding clothes. My dad's first comment was, "Where did you get that suit, Chuck?" I'm not sure he recognized Angie but seemed pleased to see her. I was careful not to talk too much about the wedding reception, which could remind him about what he was missing. We stayed about twenty minutes and I talked mostly about the nice weather, my job, and my new car, a white Pontiac 6000. I told Dad that Angie and I were headed to a party in Chicago. I felt sadness on that glorious afternoon as we left the house. I so much wanted my father to be able to share the day with us, but the best I could do was a quick visit. We jumped back into the limo and rode to the wedding reception.

Our reception at the Martinique began with an elegant cocktail reception featuring music by four violinists. We opted not to buy an expensive wedding cake so we could afford the violins in our wedding budget. It was a great call. The atmosphere the strings created was classy and romantic, and our guests enjoyed the ambiance while sipping their cocktails. Because the Martinique management was fond of Angie, we were served the restaurant's best New York strip steaks and their famous Baked Alaska dessert. And the champagne toast was free! Several of our guests said it was best wedding meal they ate. The bride and groom toasts by my brother Tom and Angie's younger sister, Kathleen, were thoughtful and funny. My brother recited a gag list of keys to a successful marriage that got lots of laughs: "May all your ups and downs come only in the bedroom."

The dance floor was crowded all night; folks of all ages rocked to the sounds of Lakefront, an outstanding wedding band we were fortunate to book due to a cancellation they had for our date. The reception was a swinging affair, as Frank Sinatra would say. Angie's brother John's best friend Terry videotaped the wedding and reception, which wasn't that common back then. Many years later, my daughter Kathleen had the VHS tape converted to a DVD so it wouldn't degrade after so many years. I haven't watched it since our first viewing together a month after the wedding. Angie was very excited to see it. Maybe I'll find the right opportunity to view it again, think back to the time Angie and I watched together, and cope with the emotion it surely will bring.

The father-daughter and mother-son dances were special, as they always are at most wedding celebrations. Angie beamed and smiled sweetly as her father, Jack, pushed her around the dance floor. The band played Angie's request, "Polka Dots and Moonbeams," sung by Stevie Wonder. Mom and I enjoyed our dance and we talked about good friends seated at her table. We did not talk about Dad. It seemed better for me to leave that subject alone and let Mom escape from it for one special night.

At the end of the reception, Angie's brothers and sisters and many of their friends stood behind Angie and me on camera on the dance floor and we belted out Tony Bennett's classic "I Left My Heart In San Francisco." Singing that song was intended to wish us bon voyage to the first stop on our honeymoon, the City by the Bay.

We arrived home in Westchester very late—about 1:00 a.m. —and fortunately we were packed for the trip. The limo was going to pick us up at 6:00 a.m. for our 9:00 a.m. flight to San Francisco. So we opened a bottle of chardonnay, sat in bed, and ripped open envelopes. We enjoyed reading fond messages on the wedding cards and separated checks from cash. I put the checks in my top dresser drawer and we took the cash with us to pay for expenses in San Francisco and Maui. We talked about the wedding most of the night and didn't get much sleep.

The flight to San Francisco left O'Hare airport on time on a sunny, calm morning which assured a smooth flight. I sat on the aisle and Angie had the window seat. The middle was empty. Angie was reading a novel. The morning edition of the *Chicago Tribune* kept me occupied. But the *Trib* sports section couldn't hold my attention and prevent me from dozing off. I snoozed most of the four-hour flight. When I woke up, I noticed that Angie was writing on a small notepad. I leaned over and saw she was practicing writing her new name, Angela Weber. I didn't say anything but appreciated how she was trying to adjust to her new life with me.

The weather in mid-September in San Francisco was gorgeous— beautiful weather in a beautiful city. We stayed at the Fairmont Hotel in the Nob Hill section. It was a classic old San Francisco hotel with bellhops in red-and-gold uniforms. It reminded me of the old television show *Have Gun - Will Travel* in which the dapper star, Richard Boone, was based in an elegant San Francisco hotel, where he would get mail and visitors seeking his services as a mercenary gunman. After check-in, we unpacked and decided to walk around the city and enjoy the bright sunny mid-afternoon weather. Angie was captivated by the city. She smiled broadly and enjoyed every minute of our walking tour. We hopped on a cable car and rode down to Fisherman's Wharf. Jumping off at the end of the line, I spotted the Buena Vista bar and grill, famous for Irish coffee. I couldn't resist introducing Angie to the landmark watering hole. The joint was crowded but we found seats at the bar and ordered two Irish coffees. She told me she liked Irish coffee. I did not know that. The bartender could tell we were newlyweds. I sat staring at Angie and said to myself "How good is this?" I guess my look was a dead giveaway to the bartender.

We had fun walking along Fisherman's Wharf popping in and out of the shops and watching sea lions sun themselves along the piers. Touristy seafood restaurants had takeout food stands and we sampled a crab-meat cocktail and shared a plastic cup of beer. The trip to the wharf wasn't complete without a visit to Alcatraz. The former max prison is a tourist attraction. The tour guide gave us a detailed history of the prison and its most notorious gangster inmates, Scarface Al Capone, Machine Gun Kelly, and Whitey Bulger. He said most of the inmates were not gangsters but persistent rule breakers who came from other prisons and required high-intensity incarceration. It was cool to walk around the cell blocks. Angie shot a playful photo of me in a cell. Unlike the weather on the wharf, it was freezing on Alcatraz Island. The wind howled and we both shivered.

During our stay we dined at several notable San Francisco restaurants, including Vanessi's on Telegraph Hill, Perry's on Union Street, the North Beach Restaurant, and the Fog City Diner. The seafood linguine at Vanessi's was outstanding. My favorite joint was the late great Washington Square Bar and Grille, known to its regulars as the Washbag. In its heyday, the bar was a bustling hangout for journalists and public relations people. I loved the place.

After three fun-filled days in the City by the Bay, we flew five hours to Maui, where we stayed at the Maui Surf. It was a reasonably priced hotel on Kaanapali Beach. The resort had a huge swimming pool staffed with cabana boys who called themselves "suntan consultants." They hawked expensive oils and lotions, which promised deep dark tans. There were no SPF ratings, however, so they were not appropriate for two people with white Irish skin that burned easily.

After just an hour poolside, Angie's freckles had popped out on her face. They were cute.

We walked a long way in the heat to the town of Lahaina, where we found an inviting bar and sipped mai tais for a couple of hours. We also bought Hawaiian shirts and Maui-logoed flip-flops. In 2023, when fire caused by sparks from broken power lines burned down most of Lahaina, my thoughts turned to those who lost everything in the fires and I also remembered those mai tais. The area is slowly recovering from the awful devastation.

One night we attended a traditional luau complete with a pig roast, tiki torches, and local ethnic dancers wearing grass skirts. Hawaiian music filled the air and the food and mai tais were served buffet style. The event was sort of a must-do while in Hawaii but neither of us thought it was worth the cost.

My favorite memory of our time in Maui was a very romantic dinner at the Kapalua Bay Club. Our table sat on a small hilltop and there were tiki torches lining both sides of the pathway down to the ocean. A mild breeze kept us cool and comfortable. We ordered a bottle of chardonnay and held hands before the wine was served. We looked into each other's eyes, smiled, and felt our deep love. It was a magic moment for both of us. After the waiter poured the wine, we drank a toast to our everlasting love. And that love was everlasting for the next thirty-three years. The dinner, which featured mahi mahi entrées and sautéed vegetables, lasted about two hours and enabled us to enjoy each other and the spectacular Kapalua scenery. I thought about the Kapalua dinner for most of the flight home.

Chapter 3

MAKING HER MARK

Angie had started her work life at the age of sixteen as a movie theater employee on the South Side of Chicago. She worked nights and performed a variety of tasks from serving popcorn to selling admission tickets. She liked working there because she made friends on the job and earned her own spending money to buy clothes. She graduated from Bogan High School in Chicago in 1976. Her parents could not afford to send her to college, so she decided to enroll at Fox Business College for secretarial training. She really had no idea about what she wanted to do career-wise, so the business college enabled her to acquire good office skills and follow an easy path to full-time employment. After graduating from Fox, Angie was hired as a secretary for Chicago-based Standard Oil Corporation. She worked in the Standard Oil Building downtown on East Randolph Street. She liked the job and the pay but hated the daily commute riding on slow CTA buses.

Angie's hatred of the commute prompted her to accept a position as the administrative assistant for the owner of the Martinique Restaurant and Dinner Theater. Her girlfriend Marion's father was the second-in-command and ran the day-to-day operation. Angie was working there when we started dating. The owner and his wife loved Angie and she frequently was given free theater tickets and was allowed to stay at the family's home in Palm Springs. I enjoyed her stories about interactions with actors and actresses who starred in performances at the dinner theater. She knew and liked actress Elke Sommer, a frequent theater performer, and told amusing stories about Forrest Tucker's drinking and Hugh O'Brian's bad hearing. She said she literally had to scream into the telephone so O'Brian could hear what she was saying. I was stunned. "Tell me Wyatt Earp isn't deaf."

Angie eventually was bored at the Martinique and knew she had to pursue a more promising career path. Marion again came through. At the time, Marion was a sales rep for Victor Technology, a supplier of calculators, adding machines, and other office products. The sales office in northwest suburban Des Plaines needed an administrator to support the office manager, an older guy named George. Marion knew George and recommended that he hire Angie as his executive secretary. She got the job but it required a tedious daily commute driving in traffic from the South Side to the northwest suburbs every day. Round trip the commute was about eighty miles. She was driving a beat-up Ford Granada with a bad heater. The Victor job gave Angie valuable corporate business experience which she parlayed into a new opportunity late in 1985 with a start-up technology company, Consumer Systems, which was based in west suburban Downers Grove. She got the job after answering a newspaper ad.

While working at Consumer Systems as a sales admin, Angie reported to the national sales manager who was an aggressive marketer and devout Mormon named Ron. Ron was almost never in the office and gave Angie a lot of responsibility in managing the company's sales operation. She excelled at her job and earned considerable respect within the company. One day Ron told Angie he was leaving Consumer Systems to take a sales position with a fast- growing, California-based software and database management company called Oracle. Ron wanted Angie to join him at Oracle as his sales administrator. The job would require commuting to downtown Chicago. We had been married two years and little did we know what a game changer this would be for Angie and me.

Angie and I talked about the pros and cons of Ron's offer. She knew Ron would be gone a lot and she would have similar responsibilities as when working for Ron at Consumer Systems. The new job offered a much better salary but Angie was hesitant about commuting every day to Chicago. She had hated the downtown commute while working at Standard Oil and didn't want to do it again. We were living in Westchester, so I told her the commute would be shorter and easier riding CTA rapid-transit trains.

While describing the job opportunity, Angie offhandedly mentioned that part of her employment package would be options on four hundred shares of Oracle stock. I said, "What? They want to give you stock options?" She didn't know what options were but I sure did from working at Abbott and knowing people who became millionaires by cashing in their options. After learning about the stock options, I begged and almost demanded that she accept Ron's offer.

Oracle proved to be a life-changing bonanza for us. Angie worked there from 1986 to 1992 and earned the respect of several executives in Chicago and at company headquarters in Menlo Park near San Francisco. Her new boss was a demanding executive VP based in Menlo Park. Twice a year, Angie traveled to San Francisco for corporate sales meetings and, in 1988, she was on the sales team that earned the top performance award. The reward was four days in Bermuda for meetings, lavish dinners, parties, awards ceremonies, and cruises. As her spouse, I could tag along and enjoy the island and its spectacular views. Our firstborn, Kathleen, was four months old and Angie's mother babysat for us.

One morning on that Bermuda trip, Angie had to attend a sales meeting so I took advantage of the free morning and played golf at the prestigious Mid Ocean Club as a guest of a retired Abbott executive. The exclusive club reeked of old money and the walls were covered with black-and-white photos of celebrities and heads of state who had visited the club, including Presidents Eisenhower and Clinton and

British Prime Minister Winston Churchill. The scenic golf course had breathtaking ocean views and challenged players with lots of sand traps and blind second shots. I played as well as I could using rented clubs and thoroughly enjoyed the round.

We shopped in Bermuda and bought some perfume and shorts, of course. Another Bermuda memory was my cocktail conversation with Oracle founder and tech industry legend Larry Ellison. He grew up in Chicago's South Shore neighborhood and was a huge NBA basketball fan. I had fun talking hoops with him and made sure he knew who Angie was. He did.

Back home, Angie's long-distance boss kept her busy processing and distributing sales reports and scheduling new business presentations and other appointments. He often called her at home and on weekends. She didn't mind and I think enjoyed being a valued asset to a top executive. She often said, "Not bad for someone without a college degree." Her efficient work didn't go unnoticed. In 1989, Angie was given five hundred additional shares of Oracle stock. After the company went public, the stock split two for one twice in the same year and our holdings were worth more than one million dollars. It was an unbelievable windfall that provided us with a substantial financial cushion that helped pay college tuitions for four children. At the time we had two young ones, Kathleen and Charlie. Even after tuition payments, we would still have a well-funded retirement account. Sadly, Angie did not live to enjoy a retirement. I'm now the beneficiary of her achievements at Oracle and often wonder how the two of us would have enjoyed spending the bounty she earned.

Angie left Oracle in 1992 about a year after our third child, Margaret, was born. The cost benefit of staying on the job dissipated from day-care costs, the personal wear and tear of commuting every day, and coming home to care for three very young children. At the time, I was traveling at least a week every month for Abbott and this, of course, put more pressure on Angie trying to juggle her job and the needs of our kids. Fortunately, we could afford living without the second income. Angie became a stay-at-home mom, a unique situation for a woman who had been continually employed outside the home since the age of sixteen.

At first, Angie enjoyed life as a full-time mom. She took the kids to local parks almost every day and to swimming pools in Palatine, where we lived at the time. Once a week, she drove to the South Side to visit her older sister, Mimi, and her three children. After Angie spent two years as a full-time mom, the recurring urge to return to the workforce and pursue a new career eventually drove her in 1995 to enroll in the nursing program at nearby Harper College. I was totally surprised by her decision because she never mentioned any interest in pursuing a career in nursing. I knew she was getting bored at home, even though she enjoyed spending her days with our children. I thought she might seek opportunities in the technology field based on her impressive experience at Oracle. She would have been an attractive candidate for any tech company seeking to upgrade its sales operations. But she answered the nursing call and followed in her sister's footsteps.

Angie excelled in the Harper nursing program, of course, and graduated with her RN degree in 1998. I hosted a large party at our home to celebrate her achievement. I was very proud of her and could tell she was pleased to be in a profession with new opportunities. The demand for RNs was strong in the Chicago market. Her first nursing job was at Northwestern Memorial Hospital working the night shift on the oncology floor. She told me it was hard work because hospitalized cancer patients are very sick and need round-the-clock nursing attention. Most people with cancer are treated as outpatients. Angie came home from work in the early morning exhausted from tending to her very ill patients and battling the reverse commute in rush hour traffic from Chicago to Palatine. I suspected she wasn't going to stay long at Northwestern, and I was right. In 1999, she was hired to be a doctor's office nurse for the Northwestern Physicians

Group in Deerfield. Angie supported two busy doctors, an internist and a dermatologist. She liked working as an office nurse and got along with the two doctors. It was far less stressful than working on the oncology floor, but the pay was less than satisfactory.

Angie liked the internist she worked with, Lee, and she pushed me to make him my primary care doctor. He still is my physician. I had a physical with him while Angie was a nurse in the practice. It's a very weird feeling being in an exam room while the nurse, who happens to be your wife, looks on as the doc examines your privates. At every visit, Lee would greet me with a joke: "What's the worst food for your sex life? Wedding cake."

After two years at the physician office practice, Angie answered an ad for a sales position with a manufacturer of motorized wheelchairs. The job required her to deliver heavy wheelchairs to handicapped patients at their homes, and also handle the required Medicaid paperwork. Two wheelchairs were stored in our garage. Our six-year-old son Michael had fun racing a wheelchair at top speed down our driveway. Angie was paid a salary draw to be charged against future sales commissions. She delivered the wheelchairs in some of the most dangerous neighborhoods in Chicago. It was risky being an attractive, defenseless woman possessing expensive medical equipment, and she strained her lower back lifting a severely obese woman into a wheelchair. I told Angie I feared for her safety and she admitted not feeling safe at many of the delivery stops.

Angie resigned from the wheelchair company in 2002, after just six months on the job. It was not a good professional or financial opportunity for her, and safety issues were a major concern. This was the second nursing-related job that wasn't right for Angie, and she began to wonder if she had made the right career decision. I stressed that her decision was sound and it might need to take time to find the right opportunity. She lay low for most of 2003, pondering what to do next, and read an article about Kelly Temporary Services and its healthcare business. Kelly placed nurses in temporary positions at companies and educational institutions throughout the Chicago area. Angie applied and was hired right away. The following week, she was dispatched to a large manufacturing plant to fill in for the company nurse who was on vacation. In another assignment that lasted several weeks, Angie traveled around the metro area giving flu shots to employees at various workplaces. She liked the flu shot gig. It was easy. And temp nursing with Kelly paid better than a full-time nursing job.

Angie worked for Kelly from 2004 to 2006. Her last assignment was at Baxter Healthcare subbing for an occupational health nurse on leave in Arizona to care for her ailing mother. Angie had been working at Baxter for two months when the chief occupational health nurse for the company offered her the nursing position full time. The woman she subbed for had resigned and relocated to Arizona. Angie believed she wasn't qualified to serve as an occupational health nurse. The chief nurse said Angie was performing the job properly and the woman whose place she was holding wasn't a trained occupational health nurse either. She told Angie Baxter would train her, and she was hired in September 2006.

This job was an enormous break. Angie hit the jackpot. She achieved her goal of becoming a medical professional working in a corporate environment, and she loved the new job.

Angie had a private clinic where she dispensed analgesics and other medications for employees with headaches, gastrointestinal distress, hangovers, and other maladies. She also treated minor workplace injuries. She took full advantage of the educational and training opportunities at Baxter. The company offered employees full tuition reimbursement for undergraduate and post-graduate degrees. While working at Baxter, Angie earned her bachelor's degree in nursing and then completed studies for a master's in nursing. She earned straight A's in the master's program. She had seen the opportunity at Baxter, seized it aggressively, and been handsomely rewarded.

Angie's story is about a young woman who was denied higher education because her parents couldn't afford to send her to college. She had a fierce desire to better herself and was determined to become a trusted and successful professional, as well as a loving mother. Angie aspired to both career and motherhood and she found ways through the years to succeed at both of them simultaneously. She beat the odds. She could have passed on the schooling and settled for secure nine-to-five administrative support jobs, for which she had a proven track record at Oracle. But that wasn't her dream. She valued education and knew it was her pathway to career achievement. She spent her weekends for two years doing homework assignments and writing papers to fulfill course requirements for her bachelor's and master's degrees. She overcame tough obstacles, climbed a huge mountain, reached the top, and planted her flag. Angie set a powerful example for our children who learned from her how to not be afraid to pursue their dreams and work hard to realize them. She is their hero—mine too.

I couldn't have been prouder of Angie for all she achieved, and told her many times. She responded by crediting me for continually encouraging her and instilling confidence. She gave me way too much credit—except for once.

While she was in the throes of obtaining her bachelor's degree, Angie had to complete an American history course and was assigned to write a paper about the presidency of Thomas Jefferson and how it shaped American democracy. We were in the process of moving from one northwest Chicago suburb, Palatine, to another, Inverness, and Angie was stressed about packing for the move and finding time to research and write the paper. I said, "Let's make a deal. If you take care of all our packing, I'll write the paper." She jumped on it and handed me the assignment sheet.

I wrote the paper in a Philadelphia hotel room while on a business trip. I Googled like crazy to get all the information I could about

Jefferson and wrote a ten-page, double-spaced paper in four hours. I emailed the document to Angie and she was ecstatic and relieved. I'm proud to say the grade for the paper was A-minus.

Chapter 4

FROM NEWLYWEDS TO PARTNERS

I divide our thirty-three-year marriage into three decades. The first covered experiencing job changes, buying a new home, caring for aging and ailing parents, trying to start a family, and eventually succeeding. The second decade covered raising and educating four children, building a successful business, spending weekends in our vacation home in Wisconsin, and adjusting to life in our forties and fifties. The third decade certainly had its highs and lows. Our children all graduated from college, there was a beautiful wedding in the family, we moved full time to our lake home in Wisconsin, and we also coped with a devastating cancer diagnosis.

A Life-Changing Career Pivot

In our first years of married life, my career at Abbott was stuck in neutral. Advancement potential was limited and I was faced with a possible career-changing decision. My options were either to seek opportunities in product marketing at Abbott and get on a different promotion track or to continue to pursue my career in public relations. If I wanted to get ahead at Abbott, I would have to leave the public relations field, but to move forward in my public relations career, I would have to leave Abbott.

The decision was difficult. I participated in a screening interview with marketing directors in the company's diagnostics division.

The division was growing rapidly so it seemed there always would be openings for product marketing positions. The outcome of the interview was disappointing. I was encouraged to apply for entry-level jobs, but the pay grades were below what I was earning in the public affairs department. I won an Abbott Presidents Award for my work in establishing a European public relations program for the diagnostics division and generated extensive favorable media coverage for several of its products. Frankly, I was somewhat insulted that I wouldn't be considered for a more attractive marketing position in one of the division's business units, considering the level of knowledge and experience I had acquired through my public relations achievements.

That disappointment led me to venture into self-employment as a freelance public relations consultant. For several years, I had thought about working for myself and pondered potential rewards that would be available to Angie and me. Angie was over the top in her enthusiasm for starting my own business. She knew it would be difficult financially for us until I was able to acquire a few clients and generate enough professional services fees to match my Abbott salary, which was $80,000. Angie never vacillated in her optimism about our future and confidence in me. She was earning in excess of $60,000 at Baxter and our only major expenses were a $2,400-per-month mortgage payment and Catholic school tuition. As she put it, "We'll have enough to get by until you start making real money." She was right. Fortunately, the business prospered early with an account from Abbott that netted $50,000 in annual fees.

I worked at home in a basement office and had to buy a new computer and a Mita combination fax machine and copier, install two phone lines for the business and fax, and subscribe to an internet service. Angie's knowledge and experience with office equipment was helpful to me in making purchasing decisions. I like to think I was a pioneer in 1993 in operating a home office enterprise. Weber and Associates Public Relations was open for business and stayed that way for the next thirty years. We survived the normal ups and downs of self-employment and I know I wouldn't have had the courage and confidence to succeed on my own without Angie's unwavering support. She never doubted me.

On the Move

After three years of marriage, Angie and I decided we needed a bigger house. The Westchester Georgian was too small and certainly would not accommodate future additions to our family. My daily commute from Westchester to Abbott in north Lake County was about forty-five minutes in good weather. So on weekends, we canvassed several communities in the north and northwest suburbs looking for the right, affordable home. In 1987, the residential real estate market in Chicago and suburbs was white-hot. Houses didn't stay on the market very long and often sold above asking price. If you liked a property you needed to make a good offer right away; otherwise, it would be gone.

An Abbott colleague lived in Palatine in northwest Cook County and recommended we work with his Realtor, Joan. When we met with her, we liked her willingness to understand our needs and likes. And it didn't take long for Joan to find a house for us. She called me on a Wednesday morning at my Abbott office and said a twenty-four-hundred-square-foot colonial home would go on the market on Friday, and it wouldn't stay available through the weekend. The listing agent was a friend of Joan's and tipped her about the new listing. I took a long lunch break and met Joan at the house, located on Ventura Drive in a quiet leafy neighborhood in north Palatine called Reseda. Joan said it was one of her favorite subdivisions in the suburb.

I instantly loved the place and knew Angie would like it. I asked Joan if Angie could see the house that night after work. I called her and said, "I think we've found the right house, but we have to move fast." As expected, Angie was thrilled with the place, so we offered the asking price of $185,000, which was a stretch for us. To our surprise, there was no counteroffer, and the owner accepted our bid. We were ecstatic about our first home purchased together.

In July 1987, we sold the Westchester Georgian in an FHA sale to a very young couple with no children. FHA required us to make several improvements to the house, including construction of a new garage to replace the structure that was falling apart. Despite the expenses incurred, we managed to earn a profit. The house sold for $75,000 and I had paid my brother $59,000 for it in 1979.

We moved into the colonial house in Palatine in August about the same time we learned Angie was pregnant with Kathleen. We also were dealing with my mother's cancer diagnosis and hospitalization. Mom knew we had purchased the house, and before we could occupy it, we drove her to see it from the outside before she was hospitalized.

The move wasn't difficult, and there was considerable empty space in the new house even after we had moved in all our furniture from Westchester. The new place had a living room with a large picture window facing the street, a narrow dining room that could fit our dining room set, and a warm, cozy family room dominated by a large wood-burning fireplace. A bonus feature was the main floor laundry room next to the family room and behind the garage. There were four bedrooms upstairs. We didn't like the small kitchen, which didn't have an eating area. There was a counter that could seat three, and we ate there most of the time. The master bedroom had a nice bathroom and our bedroom set fit perfectly. Two of the bedrooms could fit a queen bed or two double beds and a dresser. The fourth bedroom was small, and we chose to use it as an office. Another bonus was a large backyard with a patio and a couple of shade trees to shield the patio from the hot afternoon sun.

When Parents Decline

In 1998, Angie's dad's prostate cancer had advanced to the point where he had to undergo surgical castration to eliminate production of testosterone, which can fuel growth of prostate tumors. As his disease progressed, the cancer migrated to his bones and he was bedridden and in pain. Angie's heartbreak at her dad's condition was noticeable, although she tried unsuccessfully to hide it. I tried to console her and said I shared her pain. Our firstborn, Kathleen, was less than a month old when Angie brought her to her parents' home and introduced the new baby to her grandfather. I was there and it was one of the saddest experiences of my life. Angie held Kathleen close to her dad's bed so he could have a good look at her. Tears trickled down his cheeks. The emotion was overwhelming for Angie and me. This was the last time I saw her dad while he was alive. He died in April 1998.

My mother, Pat, was a longtime smoker, and in May 1987 she complained about severe back pain. On a Saturday morning, she was scheduled for imaging tests at the local hospital to determine the cause of her pain. She had so much pain that morning that she couldn't dress herself. Mom called and Angie responded right away. Angie gingerly helped her get dressed and drove her to the hospital. The test showed there was a tumor on her spine, which was causing the severe pain. She was admitted that day and had surgery to remove the tumor, but the trauma to her spine caused paralysis in her legs. The surgery did not yield significant pain relief and the doctors determined that her cancer had metastasized to her bones. Mom was given high doses of morphine and never left the hospital. She was dead forty days after being admitted. Angie was an angel of mercy during this ordeal. She visited Mom on days when I couldn't be at the hospital. My mother loved Angie and I knew her hospital visits were uplifting for her mother-in-law.

Speaking of mothers, Angie had what I thought was a complicated relationship with her mom. Angie's parents, in my opinion, were a personal obstacle she had to overcome. Her mother told Angie that after she was born they didn't name her. When the hospital staff said they needed a name for the birth certificate, her mom quickly named her after the obstetric nurse, Angela. Her brothers and sisters had Irish first names and Angie's name was Italian. No advance thought was given to how her folks would name her or if there was someone in the family she could be named after.

On several occasions, Angie's mother would make disparaging remarks about her looks. Years later, when Angie told me about what her mom said to her, I could tell her feelings were still hurt. Her mom also was critical of how Angie was raising our first two children, Kathleen and Charlie. The nearly constant negativity understandably had an adverse impact on her self-confidence as a young girl. Angie's parents had modest financial resources, so college wasn't a possible option for Angie. However, it wasn't just her. Angie's three brothers didn't attend college but her older and younger sisters graduated from nursing and podiatry schools, respectively. Her father wasn't very critical or supportive, but Angie did tell me he was happiest with her when she moved out of the house and didn't cost him any money. Parental indifference, I believe, was a major obstacle Angie was able to overcome.

Building Our Legacy

As we settled into married life, Angie and I began talking about starting a family. We had postponed trying to conceive and took three years to travel, enjoy fine restaurants, and take in sporting events. We thought it would be easy to procreate. The timing was right as I was thirty-six and Angie was twenty-eight. Her older brother and his wife had just welcomed their first child and her older sister was expecting her first. There was no family pressure coming from either side, but we certainly wanted to get started on our family. However, after a year of trying, nothing happened. So we decided to consult a fertility specialist in Chicago. During our first meeting in 1986, the doctor interviewed us about our sex life—how often, past use of contraception, and even favorite intercourse positions. The session was very awkward but the doctor did her best to keep us relaxed and give honest answers. She was satisfied with the answers to her questions.

The first treatment option was to order several different tests to see if Angie's hormone levels were sufficient for conception. The doctor drew a few vials of her blood and we scheduled a second appointment a week later to review the test results. Angie's test results were normal, with no adverse issues at all. So the focus turned to me. Was I experiencing a fertility or an impotency problem? Was my underwear too tight? The doctor told me fertility issues were common with young men, and tests could identify what the problem might be. She wanted a semen specimen for testing and handed me a small tube of Vaseline and a copy of *Playboy* magazine. I went into an empty exam room and proceeded to arouse myself and take care of business. With a sheepish look on my face, I emerged from the exam room and handed the specimen cup to a nurse. Angie couldn't help herself and snickered.

A week later, the doctor informed us that my sperm had a motility deficiency, meaning they were not swimming fast enough to fertilize one of Angie's eggs. I was referred to a urologist who ran additional tests which confirmed sperm motility was my problem. He prescribed a hormone called Clomid. The drug was prescribed to treat low testosterone, and the urologist told me it worked well for improving sperm motility. After I had been taking Clomid for about a month, Angie missed a period. She took an Abbott pregnancy test I brought home and it was positive. Angie was pregnant. We were thrilled. But our joy was short-lived. About a month later, Angie started bleeding and eventually miscarried. Her ob-gyn said the pregnancy would never be viable because there was no fetus, just a tissue sac.

Angie and I were devastated. We had not told anyone about the possible pregnancy, so no one knew about the miscarriage. We were worried that there could be trouble conceiving again. Angie's ob-gyn assured us that almost always miscarriage was not an impediment to future conception. She encouraged us to keep trying.

On March 16, 1988, Kathleen Patricia Weber was born at Hinsdale Hospital weighing eight pounds eleven ounces. And after that, Charles Gerald Weber arrived on July 18, 1989 weighing nine pounds four ounces, Margaret Mary Weber showed up on August 12, 1991 weighing nine pounds four ounces and Michael John Weber checked in on May 31, 1994 weighing an impressive ten pounds one ounce. Big babies meant Angie gained a lot of weight during every pregnancy, sometimes as much as sixty pounds. She often joked about how huge she thought she looked. With diet and exercise, she lost every ounce of the maternity weight. It was a fast-produced (six years) family with four healthy children. Clearly the fertility treatment was successful.

A New Sporting Interest

After childbearing was finished, Angie pursued a new hobby: marathon running. She became interested in running from a promotion by Dick's Sporting Goods on behalf of the Leukemia and Lymphoma Society. Runners would solicit fundraising pledges for the organization before they would compete in the races. This fundraiser was connected to the 26.2 mile Chicago Marathon set for mid-October. Angie and I attended a briefing and pledge meeting at Dick's. She wanted me to join her in signing up for the marathon, but I told her no, claiming that both of us wouldn't have time for the necessary training and still be able to handle all the school and sports activities of our children. Angie joined Alpine Runners, a Lake Zurich running group, and trained with them throughout her marathoning career. She trained on a schedule provided by the running club and dutifully trekked the prescribed number of miles on Wednesdays after work and on Saturday mornings.

Angie participated in her first Chicago Marathon on October 12, 2003 at the age of forty-five. The night before the race, she stayed overnight in a hotel with a lady who belonged to the running club. I brought the kids to the scene of the race on Sunday, and we watched the start with more than twenty thousand runners shedding their sweats and heading off to run 26.2 miles through the streets of Chicago. We wandered through the product exhibits in Grant Park and stopped in a nearby McDonald's for breakfast.

We had more than four hours to kill and eventually found seats in the bleachers near the finish line. It was fun watching runners of all ages file past us. We saw Angie finish and cheered for her lustily. We found her and hugged our congratulations in an area past the finish line where runners could get food and refreshments. Angie said was tired but felt good after the long run, and she didn't look or act exhausted or sore. She finished the race in four hours and forty minutes, placing 20,671st of 32,455 finishers. Her pace per mile was ten minutes and forty seconds. We were very proud of her for finishing as a forty-five-year-old inexperienced marathon runner. Angie felt a strong sense of achievement after finishing the race and overcoming the age and experience obstacles. I never doubted her after seeing her overcome bigger obstacles in pursuing higher education and a new career in nursing. Her training paid off and she became a devoted marathon runner.

Many people look at marathon races as bucket-list items. They complete one race and check it off the list—no more marathons. Not Angie. She jumped back into the Chicago Marathon the following year and finished the race in four hours and twenty-six minutes, placing 17,428th. She improved her performance by fourteen minutes and 3,243 finish positions.

Angie went on to compete in nine more marathons in Chicago and Milwaukee, and ran two of them with our daughters. With Kathleen, she ran the Milwaukee Marathon in 2011 and Margaret accompanied her in the Chicago Marathon in 2012. They really enjoyed their time together during their training by running around our lake on weekends and, of course, competing in the races. In 2013, Angie and Kathleen ran in the 50K Ice Age Trail Marathon in southeast Wisconsin's Kettle Morraine State Forest. That race was Angie's last marathon.

On May 18 2014, just two weeks after Angie's second surgery to remove a glioblastoma tumor, there was a special running event in Chicago honoring Angie and deputizing her supporters as members of "Angie's Army." Everyone wore army gray T-shirts with the statement "Life is tough, so is Angie" on the front and "Angie's Army" on the back. Some forty family members and friends and friends of our children showed up to run in a half marathon on Chicago's lakefront to benefit the Northwestern Brain Tumor Institute where Angie had undergone her two surgeries and had periodic MRIs and quarterly neuro oncology visits. Our group had a canopy erected to set aside space for everyone. Most of our folks didn't run the full 10K and many, like me, walked 5K. Angie was overwhelmed with the outpouring of love and support. It was a very emotional day. She was hugged constantly. Still recovering from surgery, Angie ran six miles.

Paw Prints on Her Heart

Perhaps some of the most memorable and enjoyable features of our second decade together were the canine additions to our family. In total we lived with four dogs while we were married. Angie was partial to the shih tzu breed. They are very friendly and adorable companions. According the American Kennel Club website: "Being cute is a way of life for this lively charmer. The shih tzu is known to be especially affectionate with children. Some dogs live to dig holes and chase cats, but a shih tzu's idea of fun is sitting in your lap acting adorable as you try to watch TV."[1] That sums it up very well. Our shih tzus were fun and loving pets, so much so that we often overlooked their tendency to pee inside. They are difficult to housebreak but eventually we accomplished that task.

Our first shih tzu was a black and white five-week-old female cutie we called Josie. Angie found her through a breeder in Chicago recommended by her sister, Kathleen. She was named after Angie's late Aunt Josie, who lived in Ireland. Josie was Angie's dog. She followed Angie everywhere and even sat on the ledge of our whirlpool bathtub while Angie was soaking. This pooch also was very smart. Angie trained her to fetch her slippers. She would say, "Josie, get my slippers," and the dog immediately would run up the stairs, snatch a bedside slipper in her mouth, and bring it downstairs to Angie. She was rewarded with a treat. When Angie voiced the same command again, Josie obediently fetched the other slipper.

Angie was convinced Josie needed a playmate because the dog was driving her crazy by following her everywhere. One day, Angie and our daughter Kathleen ventured into a pet store to see if there were any shih tzus available for adoption. There they fell in love with a mostly-white male shih tzu. They wanted a female, but the boy dog in the cage was so excited to see them that Angie and Kathleen couldn't resist and adopted him. We named him Miles after another deceased relative of Angie's from Ireland. Miles wasn't very intelligent, but he was the world's friendliest dog and loved going on walks. He always would let people pet him. We adopted Josie when we lived in Palatine and got Miles after moving to Inverness. There was a huge tree in the Inverness backyard, and squirrels sitting on the branches drove Miles crazy. He would race around the tree for hours looking up and barking. The squirrels would tease him by dropping acorns, which often clunked him on the head.

---

1 "Shih Tzu," American Kennel Club, akc.org, accessed March 31, 2025, akc.org/dog breeds/shih tzu.

Our kids got the bright idea to get another shih tzu in 2008 as a present for Angie's fiftieth birthday. I didn't know if Angie wanted another dog, but the kids believed she did. So our daughter Margaret took the lead and found a breeder's website showing a litter of five shih tzu puppies. She excitedly burst into my home office and urged me to check out the breeder website. I logged in and saw an adorable shot of the five puppies. Margaret said only one was a female, and she was the smallest in the litter.

Margaret convinced me to allow her to drive thirty-five miles to visit the breeder in Harvard, Illinois. Margaret was a new driver at the time so I was reluctant to allow her to make the trip, but she was persistent and I relented. Her brother Michael rode with Margaret and I gave her a signed blank personal check just in case she had to make a deposit to hold a puppy for us. About an hour later, Margaret called and said, "Dad, we have to get this dog. Look at how cute she is." The puppy was almost all white and indeed was adorable. The breeder asked for a $100 deposit to hold the dog through the weekend. She was five weeks old and would cost $600. Margaret and Michael came home excited about the new puppy and I gave them approval to get her. The following Sunday, Kathleen and Margaret drove to Harvard and bought the puppy. They also purchased a crate with a small dog bed. Kathleen hid the puppy under her coat when she entered the house and started singing "Happy Birthday" to Angie. Then she revealed the surprise present, and Angie screamed with delight. Her eyes teared as she held the puppy close to her chest and thanked everyone for the "best birthday present ever."

After a few days, we still hadn't found a name we liked. The following Saturday, seated around the kitchen table, we brainstormed lots of names and couldn't agree on one. Angie didn't have any other deceased Irish relatives she wanted to memorialize. I was pawing through the *Chicago Sun-Times* while we were kicking around possible puppy names. While looking at the obituary page, I saw an obit story about the actress Edie Adams, wife of one of my favorite comedians, the late Ernie Kovacs. He was brilliant, and his wife dutifully preserved his comedic legacy. Several early *Saturday Night Live* skits were influenced by Kovacs. Anyway, I asked what everyone thought of the name Edie. There was unanimous agreement. The little shih tzu became Edie Weber. The name was perfect. Edie was and still is very bossy and always lets you know when she wants something. As a young dog, she was very playful and loved to chase and fetch Beanie Baby toys. And, of course, Edie loved Angie and followed her around the house.

Josie had to be put down at the age of fourteen. She was badly disoriented, had trouble walking, and couldn't see very well. It was time and we knew it. Angie and I took Josie to the vet. I couldn't watch as the vet euthanized her but Angie stayed so she could say goodbye to her dear friend. We were sad but knew we had no choice.

Unbeknownst to me, Angie wanted another dog. One day she showed me a photo of a Pekingese rescue dog. The dog's name was Maximo, and he was housed at a shelter in Houston after being homeless on the city's streets. I told Angie I really didn't want another dog and besides, he was in Houston, and I didn't think Miles and Edie wanted to share our attention and affections. That argument didn't work because Angie learned the Pekingese was flown from Houston to a shelter in Fort Atkinson, close by. I wondered if he flew coach or first-class. Angie arranged for a shelter staff member to visit us to gauge our suitability to be dog parents.

Angie wasn't home when a young lady from the shelter visited. I was in a surly mood and not very friendly. I asked her what she wanted to learn about us. She responded that she needed to find out if we would be a good home for the rescue dog. I pointed to Miles and Edie standing next to me and asked, "Why don't you ask them?" She smiled and assumed that since Miles and Edie looked well cared for, our home would be a safe choice. Angie picked up Maximo at the shelter, and the first few days with him were awful. He growled and snapped at everyone, and bit my hand when I stupidly tried to pet him. Even dog-lover Angie was concerned that we might not want to keep such a nasty beast. She said the woman at the shelter told her there could be a difficult adjustment period for an abused rescue dog. She was right. It took a week for the dog to adjust, enjoy being well-fed, calm down, and become much friendlier.

The dog needed a new name instead of Maximo. I insisted that no canine should have a three-syllable name. So the name game began as it had with Edie. This time it was much easier for this dog. When I took Maximo for a walk, I noticed that he pranced when he walked. He had an arrogant strut, so I thought we should give him a stuffy British name. When I came back from the walk, I suggested that Maximo become Nigel. Angie agreed, and the once-angry Pekingese became Nigel Weber. The American Kennel Club describes a Pekinese as "charming, confident companions who develop a tight bond with their favorite human." [2] And once again, that favorite human was Angie. When she would sit in the wingback chair in our sunroom drinking her morning coffee, Nigel would climb up and sit on her lap. If Nigel was with Angie, you approached at your own risk. He was very protective and would growl and snap if you got too close.

Angie's love for dogs had a profound influence on our family life. Josie, Miles, Edie and Nigel were treated affectionately like little kids. Josie and Miles slept in our bed for a few years until Angie decided they should stay downstairs because they moved around too much in the bed. For about a week, they raised hell when banished downstairs, but they adjusted. Our dogs were a source of great joy for all of us. No matter how bad your day is going, when you get home you forget your troubles when your four-legged pals excitedly greet you. Miles lived to age eighteen, and Edie (sixteen) and Nigel (twelve) are still with me. They are wonderful companions for a guy living alone.

---

2 "Pekingese," American Kennel Club, akc.org, accessed March 31, 2025, akc.org/dog breeds/Pekingese.

Chapter 5
RAISING OUR LEGACY

Our second decade of marriage was all about parenting. By 1994, our tenth anniversary, we had four children: Kathleen, six; Charlie, five; Margaret, three; and Michael, four months. All of the births were C-sections, so we knew when the kids would be born. We did not want to know the sexes ahead of the births.

At the time, Angie had yet to embark on her nursing career so she was capably performing the duties of a full-time mom. To this day, I don't know how Angie managed caring for a new baby, a toddler, and two small children day after day, especially since I was preoccupied with managing a growing public relations consulting business, which was our lone source of income. Working at home amid sometimes hectic everyday family activities often posed challenges to stay focused on work.

Almost as soon as we moved into the Palatine colonial home, Angie began contemplating improvements she wanted. For instance, we didn't like the small kitchen, which didn't have an eating area. There was a counter that could seat three, and we ate there most of the time. She really liked the house and the neighborhood, and knew the improvements she was thinking about would improve the home's utility, overall appeal, and value. Her first priority was to construct an addition on the back of the house that would provide a sunroom and an eating area extended from the kitchen. Construction began about four years after we moved in. Angie designed the sunroom with help from the builder we hired. She liked cathedral ceilings and designed the sunroom to accommodate one. The cathedral ceiling fit well with the large windows on the back wall. The kitchen eating area was a step up from the sunroom with a large window on the back wall, and could fit a table that sat six.

Angie's judgment and good taste were evident in the finished construction. The sunroom was very bright with lots of sunlight that illuminated the white walls and ceiling. We bought a large, deep, flowered sofa with a matching wingback chair. It was a lovely room, perfect for relaxing, napping, and reading. Ample floor space allowed enough room for our little ones to crawl about. We ate our meals in the new kitchen eating area almost every day. It was a bright, convenient, and comfortable space, and a home improvement success for Angie.

We received numerous compliments from family, friends, and neighbors for the sunroom. After the project was completed, we bought a hot tub for the patio, which we could access from the sunroom. It was the perfect arrangement—a bright relaxing sunroom next to a soothing spa.

Angie, however, had another home improvement scratch to itch. She never liked the bathtub in the master bedroom, and believed we needed a larger bedroom that would enable us to allocate more of the existing space upstairs for our four kids. The girls had a bedroom with two double beds and the boys slept in bunk beds in the third bedroom. Angie's idea was to build a new master bedroom and bath on top of our garage. There was plenty of space.

So in 1998, we hired a contractor who was the husband of a sixth-grade teacher at the Catholic school our kids attended. His name was George, and he was highly recommended. Angie liked him, and George was smart enough to know that Angie would be the boss on this project. George and his crew were fun to work with and had good ideas. When the project was complete, we basically had a new upstairs. Our master bedroom and bath were on the south end of the floor. The room had a cathedral ceiling, of course, and large windows, and the master bath had a large Jacuzzi tub for Angie. She soaked in it every night. I could not believe how hot her bathwater was. Angie's entire body below the neck was beet red when she climbed out of the tub.

When the addition was finished, we moved the girls into our old bedroom space and kept the boys in the third bedroom with the bunk beds. The tiny fourth bedroom stayed as an office that Angie used. It had a desk and a computer terminal for Angie to get emails from Oracle.

So with all the improvements, one would think we would have stayed in the remodeled home for many years. Nope. Two factors drove our decision to sell the Palatine house. We found a huge whitewashed brick home in Inverness, about three miles from the Palatine colonial, with very large rooms on the main floor and upstairs and a huge, twenty-five-hundred-square-foot basement that was a perfect space for our teenagers to host their friends; play pool, Ping Pong and darts; and enjoy watching movies in a large home theater. The other factor was that Angie and I preferred the excellent high school on the south side of Palatine that our kids could attend if we moved.

We sold the Palatine house for $400,000 in 2001 after paying $185,000 in 1987. The improvements, however, cut into the profit, so we might have netted $25,000 on the sale. We paid $880,000 for the Inverness home. Unlike our previous moving day, this one was a disaster. The seller was a jerk, an asshole's asshole. He insisted on delaying the closing because of a stupid legal technicality. While we impatiently and angrily waited to finish the closing, the movers sat on the clock in their loaded truck full of our stuff in front of the Palatine house. We paid a tidy sum for their overtime. We closed in the late afternoon, and Angie refused to shake the seller's hand. The movers worked in the dark and finally completed the job at 10:00 p.m. There was no time to arrange furniture, so we were forced to skip work the next day to get the place partially in shape. That night, we put our mattress on the floor in the master bedroom and slept there.

Angie, of course, had ideas for improving the Inverness home, although the hefty sale price did not leave us much of a budget for improvements. But that didn't limit Angie. She hit a big sale at a Sears furniture warehouse and bought two large chests of drawers, which fit nicely in the family room and foyer. She also grabbed a serving table for the dining room. It was quite a haul. Next, it was time to upgrade the kitchen decorating. Angie hired husband-and-wife painters who specialized in faux-finish painting. The couple had done a nice job for us in the Palatine sunroom. Faux-finish painting creates texture and nuance to replicate the look and feel of other surfaces like suede or marble. Angie hired the painters to refinish the kitchen walls. It was a laborious and expensive job, but the final product was a very attractive muted floral design.

The enormous basement gave our home a reputation for being the best party house for high schoolers. In the twelve years we lived there, all four kids hosted numerous parties, and we made sure we always were home when the kids hosted their friends. Parents would call us to make sure we would be home. As the kids arrived, Angie would confiscate car keys because we didn't want to be responsible for kids taking off from our home to go to another party their parents didn't know about, which might have alcohol available.

Our daughter Margaret's parties were legendary. She had an army of girlfriends who would come to the house in the afternoon to hang party decorations. One New Year's Eve, she hosted ninety guests. Angie and I had no idea that many teenagers would show up. The doorbell kept ringing and kids kept coming. Their shoes were piled high in the front foyer.

The craziest party story stems from an incident during one of Michael's gatherings. A girl fell through the wall in the home theater next to the big screen. She left a large hole in the drywall. Angie and I were away for the weekend and didn't know about Mike's party. The next day, Mike and two of his friends went to Home Depot to learn how to fix the drywall. A very helpful sales person advised the boys about the supplies they would need and how to patch the hole. Every night for week, Michael and his pals worked on fixing the drywall. The finished patch job was nearly perfect, and they matched the paint so well we couldn't tell it wasn't the original color. Angie and I were home for the entire repair, but didn't go downstairs because we thought the boys were watching sports or movies in the home theater. When we sold the house in 2012, the buyer's home inspector didn't find anything wrong in the home theater. Angie I finally learned about the drywall episode when the kids told us about it while we were drinking months later at a beachfront tiki bar in Costa Rica. All we could do in response was laugh and express our amazement at how Michael and his buddies were able to pull off that repair job.

Angie and I enjoyed a fairly active social life while living in Palatine and Inverness and belonging to the Catholic parish, where our kids attended school. For three years, I was president of the parish school board. Most of our social circle were the parents of our kids' friends. That's a common way to meet people in the suburbs because you are frequently attending school and athletic events.

Kathleen and Charlie graduated from St. Theresa School in Palatine, Margaret completed six grades and graduated from the public junior high school, and Michael completed three and finished at the junior high. Kathleen thrived at St. Theresa and was a favorite of many of the teachers, who were mostly middle-aged women. Charlie did not fare as well as Kathleen. Boys at the school would have benefitted from some male teachers because the women on the faculty clearly favored the girl students. Charlie felt he was picked on, and I believe he was because he often was in trouble. His best experiences at the school came from playing on the basketball team. He was one of the best players and I was the head coach. Our team had winning records every season from fifth to eighth grade.

Margaret and Michael prospered at the junior high school. Both made nice friendships, and Margaret was the morning news anchor for the school's closed-circuit television station. Michael's departure from St. Theresa was engineered by Angie. His third-grade teacher one day punished him for wearing ankle-length socks. She said the socks were not appropriate to wear in school. She also wrote some nasty comments on one of his homework papers—bad move because she angered Angie, who confronted the teacher face-to-face in her classroom. Voices were raised and Angie stormed out of the classroom after telling the teacher what she thought of her. After that incident, Angie pulled Michael and Margaret from St. Theresa and moved them to award-winning Sundling Junior High School.

High school was a good experience for all four children. District 211 is one of the best for academic excellence in the state of Illinois. Our kids attended Fremd High School in Palatine. Kathleen played basketball and lacrosse, earned straight A's, was inducted into the National Honor Society, and graduated with honors. Charlie played soccer and basketball and ran on the track team. Soccer was his best sport, and he was an all-conference selection his senior year. Charlie had to work hard at his studies as a B student. On the day report cards came in the mail, Charlie and I were together in the kitchen making hamburgers for dinner. I asked if we should open the report cards, and he said yes. We first looked at his card and the grades were good—all B's and one A. Nice job, Charlie. Then we opened Kathleen's: all A's. Charlie protested. "It's not fair. She does her homework in front of the TV and still gets all A's."

Margaret lettered in both cross-country and track. She excelled as a long-distance runner. She was the conference champ in cross-country as a sophomore and finished the top half of the field in the statewide cross-country meet as a senior. Michael played hockey and made the conference all-star teams as a sophomore and senior. He won the offensive player of year award as a senior. Both Margaret and Michael were average students earning B's and C's.

In 2000, Angie and I joined Biltmore Country Club in North Barrington. I played golf there two—sometimes three—times a week, and we attended many of the club's social events. We were popular with the members and enjoyed socializing at club events. One member asked me, "How does a schmuck like you have such a gorgeous wife?" The highlight of the club's social season was the members gala Christmas party. Men wore tuxes and the ladies were gowned in stylish long dresses. Angie looked forward to this event every year and her class and beauty were on display for everyone. There was one couple at the club with whom we developed a close relationship and had numerous dinners together. These good friends moved to Arizona eight years ago and were very supportive visiting us at home in Angie's final days in 2017. I still maintain close contact with them. We connect whenever I'm in Arizona.

One of the many benefits of belonging to the club was feasting at the lavish brunches served on New Years Day, Easter and Mother's Day. We would bring all four kids, and they would eagerly attack the bountiful buffet and dessert table. Charlie also brought dates to the club for dinner. He couldn't pay from his own pocket but was able to sign my name to the check. (Nice deal.) We stayed at the club until 2010 when the cost of having three children in college meant the club no longer fit in the family budget. We hated to leave but had no choice.

Life at the Lake

When Angie was growing up on Kirkland Street in the Bogan neighborhood, her two best friends, Kate and Marilyn, lived next door and across the street. Marilyn's parents were teachers and they had a summer home in southwest Michigan. Angie stayed at their summer place frequently, and for many years she dreamed about having a lake home of her own. In 1992, Angie and I discussed buying a lake home in Wisconsin. She talked about how much fun she had in Michigan. She wanted our kids to be able to swim, fish, and go on boat rides on weekends every summer. I had never had a summer home experience as a kid. Our family would spend a week a year at Lake Como in southern Wisconsin.

On a very cold Friday night in January, we packed our three kids into the minivan and drove five hours to Door County to look at lakefront properties. We rented a condo for the weekend. On Saturday, we looked at five different lake homes and only liked one. The Realtor said the owner was motivated to sell. During dinner at a quiet supper club, we weighed the pros and cons of buying the house. We decided against a purchase mainly because Door County was too far from home, and we were unlikely to be able to spend much time there. We focused our attention on properties that were no more than a three-hour drive from home.

In March, we found a cozy place on a small lake called Alpine Lake in Wautoma. The house was rustic: it had three bedrooms, a small kitchen, and a screened patio. The lot was deep and the shoreline was rocky and weedy. The water wasn't very deep close to shore, so it was safe for Kathleen and Charlie to wade into. I bought a second-hand rowboat with a trolling motor, and took the kids for short boat rides. We spent every other weekend at the lake house, and, on occasion, Angie's sisters and brothers would make the trip from Chicago to visit. After three years in Wautoma, Angie decided the house was too small for our growing family (Angie was pregnant with Michael). Alpine also was a no-wake lake, meaning there could be no speedboats, tubing, water-skiing, and wave runners. We knew our kids would want to participate in all the water sports in a few years.

We wanted to find a lake property closer to home that would be a convenient drive every weekend. We drew a circle on a map of Wisconsin that would cover an area about a two-hour drive from home. Right away, we knew that beautiful and prestigious Lake Geneva was way out of our price range, and we focused on Whitewater Lake in Walworth County, which was ninety minutes from home. On a Saturday in mid-summer, Angie and I and our now four kids (Michael was born on May 31) met with a Realtor named Mary who showed us around Whitewater Lake. We were very impressed with the seven-hundred-acre lake. It was quite scenic and isn't a boring big oval. It is three separate lakes that were drained into one with lots of mature trees on the shoreline and high bluffs upon which sit very attractive homes. Mary asked if we wanted to see a few of her listed homes. We told her to limit the viewing to houses under $200,000.

What we learned quickly is that you base your decision to buy a lake home on the quality of the shoreline and the scenic view. You can always upgrade and remodel a house, but nothing can be done to change the shoreline or lake view. We looked at some very nice homes, but eliminated them right away because they were on elevated lots that would be dangerous for little kids playing in the yard. There were two houses with modern interior decorating that Angie really liked, but she agreed the elevated lots were deal killers. Some lots had huge drops.

At the end of the search, Mary showed us two properties that were not on elevated lots. One was on Lakeshore Drive and had a main floor and downstairs walkout level and a very nice kitchen, which Angie liked. It had three bedrooms, all on the walkout level. The yard sloped down to the lake and there was a nice view. It was not an attractive structure and one drawback was that the house had a flat roof, which I didn't like because it would accumulate snow and be prone to leaks. The second house was on Krahn Drive on the far west end of the lake. Like the previous house, it had a main floor and walkout level. The owner was a widow in her seventies named Jeanette who lived in

Florida most of the year and came to Wisconsin for a month or two in the summer to visit her friends. The house had been listed for more than a year, and Mary the Realtor had convinced her to lower the price to $210,000.

This house had a large screened porch on the main floor facing the lake. That feature was very attractive for both of us. We imagined ourselves spending summer evenings on the porch drinking wine and listening to music after the kids were in bed. The next day, Sunday, after church we talked about the houses we were considering. We agreed that Whitewater Lake was where we wanted to be. And we knew we had to make a decision fairly soon because the properties would likely attract other offers by the next weekend. Working in our favor, however, was a glut of more than twenty homes for sale on Whitewater Lake. It was a buyer's market. A real estate tax increase had passed in a referendum a year earlier to build a new high school. As a result, folks who were leaning toward selling pulled the trigger and put their properties on the market because they didn't want to pay higher taxes to fund a school they wouldn't use.

Angie was leaning toward the house with the nice kitchen on Lakeshore Drive, and I wanted to buy the widow's place on Krahn Drive. We were at an impasse. Neither one of us would agree to change our minds. So, I had an idea about how we could break the tie. On a slow August Friday, I left work at Abbott in the early afternoon and drove to Whitewater Lake to reinspect the two properties without the Realtor. I wanted to further examine the shorelines and close-in lake depth. The first stop was the Lakeshore house. No one was around. I removed my shoes, socks, slacks and dress shirt and waded into the water. After about ten steps, I fell into the lake and was totally submerged thanks to a steep drop. The water close to shore was about six feet deep—no way that would work for little kids. To me, that was a deal killer. Next, I had to check the shoreline and close-in water depth at the widow's house.

I didn't bother to put my clothes back on because it was a very short drive to Krahn Drive. I parked in the driveway and walked nearly naked past the house and down to the shoreline. I waded into the water and kept walking farther and farther before the water level reached my upper chest. Perfect. No big drops or deep water close to shore. This was the right choice for us. When I got home, Angie couldn't believe what I had done, but she was grateful to learn about the sharp difference in close-in water depth between the two properties. We agreed to submit an offer to the widow.

I called the Realtor and said we wanted to buy. She told me that Jeanette preferred to sell to a young family, and if we made a reasonable offer, she probably would accept it. She did not want to hold onto the house for another winter. We made a low-ball offer, and Mary advised me to up it. Our next offer was $178,000, and the owner came down from $210,000 to $195,000. We countered at $189,000 and she accepted.

Angie and I were thrilled about the lake home purchase and knew it would be wonderful for years of family fun. Our children basically grew up at the lake house. Michael was four months old when we took occupancy. Summer after summer from 1994 to 2016, our family, relatives, and friends gathered at the lake to enjoy boating, tubing, and wake boarding as well as tasty entrées from the Weber Genesis Grill. We had a twenty-foot deck boat with a six-cylinder inboard motor which was perfect for taking the kids tubing and wake boarding. Every weekend we had lengthy sessions on the lake using the deck boat to pull our kids, their cousins, and their friends in the two-person tube. The boys enjoyed when I made sharp turns, forcing them to fly off the tube into the water. Charlie and Michael eventually graduated to wake boarding and preferred it to tubing. I didn't take long for them to become skilled wake boarders.

We also had a twenty-four-foot pontoon boat that Angie piloted all the time. The pontoon was what we called our booze cruiser. When we were finished with the tubers and wake boarders by midafternoon, Angie and I and our guests for the weekend would board the pontoon with a full cooler of beverages and cruise around the lake for a couple of hours. On weekends with no guests, Angie and I would cruise by ourselves before dinner and chat aimlessly. We thoroughly enjoyed our time together on the water for many years. Sunday nights were special for us. We would enjoy wine on the porch, stay overnight, and get up early. Angie would head to her job at Baxter and I went to my home office. We looked forward to our Sundays alone. The kids would go home late on Sunday afternoons on most weekends. Kathleen was their driver.

On one of our Sunday evenings at the lake, Angie and I talked about retiring someday at the weekend home. But we knew we could not live full time in the current house. The rooms and kitchen were too small and the appliances and furnace would need to be replaced. So we talked about remodeling the house, and our painter, who lived across the lake from us, recommended a contractor for whom he worked on a regular basis. The contractor, Tom, met us at the house on a Saturday morning toward the end of the summer and brought his architect. Tom and the architect thoroughly inspected the house, measuring floors, wall space, and ceiling height.

We described all the improvements we wanted to make. Tom told us he could do the remodeling job in accordance with our specifications, but warned that we would not be satisfied. The remodeled home wouldn't be what we really wanted. He convinced us to demolish the house and build a new home. Would it be the house of our dreams? I believe Angie was thinking that way. Tom said he would prepare blueprints and a construction plan and budget. We told him we weren't ready to move yet and that it might be at least a year before we could start building.

In August 2012, Angie and I drove Michael to Xavier University in Cincinnati to start his freshman year. On our way home, our Realtor called and said we had an offer on the Inverness house. It was less than we paid for the place, but since it had been on the market for eighteen months, we decided to cut our losses and accept the offer. It was a loss of about $150,000. Ouch! But that sale cleared the path for us to move full time to Whitewater. We closed on Inverness on Halloween, moved to the lake house, and rented a large storage unit to store the furniture we moved from Illinois.

After a couple of months in the lake house, we were convinced that Tom was right and we should build a new house. We learned there was no insulation on the walkout level where I worked. I had to wear one of my bulky Irish sweaters to stay warm. We later found out the house was not secured to the foundation, which made it very easy to tear down. A big wind could have blown the structure off the foundation.

Before the holidays, we finalized blueprints with Tom and his architect, and construction would begin in February. Tom said it was good timing because many of the carpenters and other tradesmen he hired were looking for work, and he could have ten workers on the job for most of February and March. The men worked in some awfully cold weather. It took only eight months to finish construction of the new house, and we were delighted with the quality of the work.

The main floor is a great room that has a family room, kitchen, and sunroom. The kitchen has top-of-the-line appliances. A screened porch is next to the family room through a sliding glass door. Upstairs are four bedrooms. The master bedroom is huge: it has a king-size bed and hanging light fixtures, and was designed by Angie. The master bathroom has a walk-in shower and a Jacuzzi bathtub. The walkout basement level has a beautiful stone floor, a bar, and a large sectional sofa, which is perfect for watching sports on the seventy-inch television. There is a large flagstone patio adjacent to the lower level. We furnished our new home with the furniture from Inverness, which wasn't aesthetically compatible with a lake house, but we were planning to buy new furniture within a year. Fate intervened. Angie was diagnosed with terminal brain cancer on October 30, which was the day after her fifty-fifth birthday. Two years after Angie died, I replaced the Inverness furniture. I think she would have approved.

Wedding Bells

Our oldest daughter Kathleen and her now-husband Paul had been together for seven years and lived in Milwaukee. Kathleen graduated with a business degree from Marquette in 2010 and worked at Rockwell International in procurement and supply chain management. Paul graduated from Indiana University with a degree in accounting and worked for the State of Wisconsin Department of Revenue. They lived together in the trendy Brady Street neighborhood.

After her first brain-tumor surgery on November 1, 2013, Angie asked Kathleen if she and Paul were planning to get married. Kathleen said they were and Angie said she was pleased and would hold them to it. Kathleen read between the lines and knew they should move quickly before Angie's disease worsened. And it did. She had a tumor recurrence in May that required a second craniotomy, which fortunately was successful in removing the tumor. She made a full recovery. Kathleen and Paul set the wedding date for October 14, 2014. They moved fast in making arrangements and were fortunate to take advantage of some cancellations. They booked the historic Pfister Hotel for the wedding reception and hired the best wedding band in Milwaukee, Velocity. The wedding ceremony was scheduled at St. Raymond's Church in Shorewood, just north of Milwaukee. A newly ordained priest from Nigeria would preside at the ceremony. It would be his first wedding.

Angie, Kathleen, and Margaret went dress shopping in June at two specialty shops in Milwaukee. Angie told Kathleen on the phone that the dress she selected was "almost white." Well, the dress indeed was pure white, so the mother of the bride wore white at her daughter's wedding. She was the star of the event next to Kathleen. Our guests were amazed at how beautiful Angie looked just four and half months following brain surgery. Her hair had grown back to an attractive short style which she dyed blond. She thought her short hair would look better blond instead of her natural red. She was right. I liked her new look.

Kathleen wanted to be married in St. Raymond's Church because it had the longest center aisle in the Milwaukee area. I enjoyed walking down every foot of that aisle arm in arm with her. The short Nigerian priest said a very entertaining wedding Mass. You could tell he was proud to be presiding and felt affection for Kathleen and Paul. He sang a couple of hymns during the ceremony while holding his arms in the air. It was part Catholic nuptials and part *The Lion King*.

One summer afternoon in 2014 back at the lake, Charlie, Michael, and l had burgers at a bar on Turtle Lake called Snug Harbor Inn. Over our pre-meal beers we pondered how we could put a Wisconsin spin on Kathleen's wedding. We hit on the idea to hire the famous Milwaukee Brewers sausage racers to make an appearance during the cocktail reception. Michael called the Brewers and learned that each sausage character could be hired for two hours for $100. He hired the hot dog and bratwurst characters. At the reception, Michael was in charge of the sausages. When the actors arrived at the Pfister, they called Mike, and he escorted them to his hotel room to change into their sausage outfits. Michael staged it perfectly. He walked into the cocktail party with Hot Dog and Bratwurst and the crowd cheered wildly. Several of our guests posed for photographs with the sausages. Our family posed with the sausages, too, and that shot is framed and sits on a sofa table in the upstairs hall. When the sausages walked in, Kathleen turned toward me from the receiving line and pointed with a smile expressing her approval.

The band Velocity kept the dance floor jumping. They played a wide array of popular hits that kept the party lively and fun. Many guests said this was the best wedding band they had heard. Angie was radiant throughout the evening. She posed for pictures with seemingly every guest. She kicked off her shoes and danced barefoot. I was thrilled about how much fun Angie had at the wedding. It was the highlight of the year for her and a wonderful distraction from thinking and stressing about her brain cancer.

THE LIGHT SHE GAVE

One of my favorite shots showing Angie's radiant smile

In her forties and fifties, Angie ran 11 marathon races

The pontoon captain enjoys a frosty margarita

A beautiful bride awaits her wedding ceremony on Sept. 15, 1984

Happy Birthday! Angie called Edie her best birthday present ever

Aug. 25, 2009: Nothing better than dinner at an elegant Paris bistro

THE LIGHT SHE GAVE

Aug. 16, 2016: We enjoyed the captivating Alaska scenery

The love of my life

THE LIGHT SHE GAVE

The sisters: Kathleen (left), Mimi (center) and Angie at formal charity fund raiser

Angie with Kathleen and Charlie

THE LIGHT SHE GAVE

Costa Rica, December 2014: The family enjoyed balmy
outdoor dining every night of our stay

The family pauses on a hillside during a Costa Rica hike

Chapter 6

MILES OF MEMORIES

Throughout our marriage we were fortunate to take numerous vacations with and without children. Some trips described in this chapter are special memories because they commemorate major milestones in my life with Angie, such as our trip to Paris for our twenty-fifth wedding anniversary and our delightful visits to Costa Rica and partying with our children.

Ireland

The first major trip was an excursion in August 1985 to Angie's parents' homeland on the west coast of Ireland in County Kerry. Angie's father (Jack), mother (Hannah), and sister (Kathleen) accompanied us. We landed at Shannon Airport on a Sunday morning and rented a car. Jack was the driver because he alone knew how to navigate a vehicle on Irish roads driving on the opposite side of the street. We were staying at a family friend's beach house in the seaside town of Ballyheigue, which was Hannah's birthplace. Our arrival was heralded in the local newspaper, and word around town was the wealthy relations from America were visiting. Angie had been to Ballyheigue when she was a teenager and spent time with cousins on her mother's side and some family friends. She had fond memories and fun stories about her stay. I met a few of her cousins and a dairy farmer named Willy, who laughed a lot while he constantly talked and enjoyed his whiskey. I couldn't understand a word he said.

The beach house had big windows and low ceilings, and we slept on a cot in the main room. One night, we quietly made love under the covers.

The gathering spot for the town was the pub in the White Sands Hotel. It served as our night spot while Angie and I were in Ballyheigue, which was three days, and it seemed like Jack knew everyone in the pub. Newspaper reports of our visit brought out folks in the town who knew Angie's mom and dad. The pub was packed and very loud every night. Jack spoke with a noticeable brogue, but at home I had no difficulty understanding him. In his native Ireland, however, the dialect was unintelligible to me. I was bar side with him and three of his friends one night. They bought all the drinks. There was no way I could follow the conversation. They spoke English but talked so fast it might as well have been Mandarin. I just nodded my head and smiled. The White Sands pub also was the site of my first taste of Irish whiskey. It was a spirit called Paddy and I liked it. In my opinion, Paddy is the smoothest Irish whiskey on the market. For years, Paddy wasn't sold in the United States, so if a friend was traveling to Ireland—which many people I knew at Abbott did regularly—I would ask to bring home a bottle for me.

Jack hailed from the adjacent town of Ballybunion, famous for the Ballybunion golf links. He drove Kathleen and me to the golf course for a round but he didn't want to play. Kathleen and I walked eighteen holes with a caddy who effortlessly carried two rented golf bags on the windswept course. We thoroughly enjoyed our Irish golf experience. I wasn't sure how Jack passed the time while we were golfing, but he met us in the pub after we finished our round. I was surprised he didn't want to play with us because he loved golf and played the course regularly when he caddied there. What I didn't know—and I don't believe Angie knew—was that Jack had prostate cancer and he postponed treatment for it until after the Ireland trip. The cancer took his life two years later.

After we had stayed in Ballyheigue for three days walking the beach and visiting relatives and friends, it was time to see more of Ireland. Jack drove Angie, Kathleen, and me to the railroad station in nearby Tralee. It was a cold morning. We boarded the train and settled in for the three-hour ride to Dublin. Just as the train was about to pull out of the station, the conductor stepped into our car and announced there were mechanical problems and we had to switch to a train without food or beverage service. Some passengers moaned and the conductor replied, "As the nuns would say, offer it up." I had to laugh because I recalled nuns saying exactly that at the Catholic grade school I attended.

Our time in Dublin involved a lot of walking and sightseeing, visits to numerous pubs, and an afternoon at a horse racing track. We walked up and down O'Connell Street over the River Liffey and popped in and out of many shops. Cigar shops sold Cuban cigars, which are still illegal in the U.S. I was eager to buy some, despite the steep prices. I couldn't resist and purchased a box of twenty-five Cubans and asked the store owner how I could sneak the cigars past U.S. customs. "Not to worry," he said. "I know the best way to get them through baggage searches." From underneath his display counter, he pulled out a tin container with an image of Blessed Virgin Mary on the lid. The empty container previously held a statue of Mary. "They never search religious packages. You'll be okay." The Cubans made it past customs and I enjoyed smoking them on my patio.

The three of us were tired from all the walking and found an appealing pub in central Dublin. I sat at the bar flanked by Angie and Kathleen. Right away we attracted attention. Of course we did. I was sitting between two beautiful Irish redheads and three friendly men meandered over to talk to us. They were partners in a Dublin restaurant. The conversation was lively and the guys offered to show us their favorite night spots in Dublin. We accepted and met them later at their favorite pub. There we met several of their friends. They wanted to know all about Chicago and we accommodated them with stories about the large Irish population on Chicago's South Side and its best bars; we talked about legendary Irish politicians in the city, and related stories about Al Capone and other famous gangsters. The night flew by and the pub closed at 11:00 p.m., which we thought was way too early. "No problem," said one of our new friends. He told us about an after-hours place nearby, and we promptly headed there. After forty years, I can't recall any of their names but remember them fondly for the fun we had.

Understandably, we slept late the next morning and I woke up with a pounding headache. I lost count of the number of Guinness pints I drank at six. Angie and Kathleen felt much better than me. It was Saturday and on our schedule for the day was a trip to Phoenix Park Race Course. Horse racing is very popular in Ireland and we looked forward to enjoying an Irish racing experience. We were not disappointed.

It was Best Dressed Ladies' Day at the track and dozens of stylishly clad women paraded on the wet track in heels. It was a combination fashion show and beauty pageant. It was fun to watch but we quickly got down to the business of betting on the races. Bookmaking is legal in Ireland and regulated by the government. At an Irish race track, bettors can place wagers at the track's tote window, as we do at U.S. tracks, or you can place your bets with independent bookies who operate their stands on the concourse. You usually get better odds with the bookies, but if you win a race, be sure to cash your ticket right away. If a bookie is having a bad day, he can close shop for the day. Since bookmaking is regulated in Ireland, you can cash your ticket at any betting office in the country. Angie had a winner that paid six to one, and I cashed a couple of tickets as well. It was a fun and slightly profitable day.

The remaining days on our Ireland tour took us to Waterford, Cork, and Killarney. We visited the impressive Waterford Crystal factory store and saw how craftsmen created gorgeous glassware, lamps, vases and trophies. Cork was the next stop, home to the famous Blarney Stone.

On the train to Cork, Angie and Kathleen read their books and I engaged in conversation with two tweed-clad retirees who were studying racing forms. I interrupted and asked about the racing scene in Ireland. The two gents told me that in Ireland, horse-race meets move around the country from week to week, and the two friends took advantage of free transportation provided by the government for retirees. They went to various tracks a few times a week. When we stepped off the train in Cork, I told the two old-timers I enjoyed talking with them. We shook hands and one said, "It's time for a pint."

The next morning, we headed to Blarney Castle and stood in a long line waiting to kiss the Blarney Stone. It's a ridiculous tradition in which you climb to the top of the castle's tower and lean backward to kiss the stone above you. The legend claims that kissing the Blarney Stone rewards you with the gift of eloquence. I wasn't very talkative after that long trek up the tower stairs and smooching the stone.

In Killarney we stayed in a dumpy bed-and-breakfast in which the rooms were located above a busy pub. It was not comfortable, but we dealt with it and managed to get a decent night's sleep.

After walking the streets of Killarney, we stopped at a nursing facility that was home to Angie's Aunt Nora, who had been committed to the home at a young age. Neither Angie nor Kathleen could tell me why Nora was forced to spend her life there. It seemed she was mentally ill, but I couldn't tell for sure. She was Jack's sister, and Angie told me the family hardly talked about her. We sat with Nora for about a half hour. She was quiet and withdrawn, but recognized Angie and Kathleen from photos she had. It was sad visiting someone living a wasted life.

Killarney concluded our tour. We returned to Tralee where Jack picked us up and drove back to Ballyheigue. Angie and I were alone for a while back at the seaside house. She looked at me and said, "I feel like I belong here. Everyone looks like me." She was sincere, and I think she may have been scarred as kid from being teased about her red hair and freckles. I could tell how happy she was being in Ireland. The thought crossed my mind that maybe we should move there.

Our last stops for the trip were on the west coast: Lahinch and Galway. At Lahinch, we scaled up to view the beautiful Cliffs of Moher. It was a tough climb on the rain-soaked, slick, muddy turf. We stayed for about twenty minutes and shot lots of photos. After seeing the cliffs, we stopped at the Lahinch seaside golf links and checked out the pro shop. I grabbed a scorecard but didn't buy anything. Jack said he had played the course many years ago, and it was very challenging to battle the winds on the seaside links. He had been a good golfer when he was younger.

In Galway, we toured the city and stayed in a comfortable bed-and-breakfast. I remember that the best meal we had on the entire trip was at a seafood restaurant on the coast. A highlight was stopping in the men's clothing store that served as the outfitter for the cast of the movie *The Quiet Man*. There were large black-and-white photos on the walls of actors John Wayne, Maureen O'Hara, and Barry Fitzgerald working on the movie set. I bought a bulky off-white knit Irish sweater at the shop. I still have that sweater, and yes, it fits me after forty years.

Ireland was our first long vacation since our Hawaiian honeymoon. We left the country with lots of wonderful memories of the sights we visited, the friendly people we met, and, of course, the lively pubs.

Costa Rica

Years later, our favorite family vacation spot was Costa Rica. Angie made the astute decision in 2009 to forgo buying Christmas presents for the kids and invest money we would spend on clothes and other gifts they didn't need on warm-weather vacations during the holidays, even though it is the most expensive time of the year to fly anywhere.

We took four trips to different parts of the country (Jaco, Tamarindo, and Samara). We chose Costa Rica because it is safe and the weather is very warm in Central America in December. Everyone wanted to escape the cold. The kids were in high school and junior high.

On our first trip in 2009 we were supposed to stay at a resort in the Arenal rain forest near a volcano. We were excited to tour the rain forest and marvel at species of colorful birds, monkeys, and other animals. The warm springs for bathing also were very appealing. However, our itinerary was disrupted when our Delta flight to the San José airport on Christmas Day was delayed more than two hours due to mechanical problems that required an aircraft switch. The replacement plane had a smaller seating capacity, which required all passengers to be assigned new seats. It was chaos and took forever for the gate agents to find seats for everyone. The lengthy delay caused us to miss our connection in Atlanta to San José and we were stuck in Atlanta until morning. Christmas dinner was fast food at the airport's sports bar. The lesson from this experience was to never fly on Christmas because airline employees who knew what they were doing wouldn't be working that day.

The airline offered an allowance for an overnight hotel stay but for only one room. Here was where Angie went into action. She went to the customer service counter and raised hell, insisting that we needed two rooms to accommodate our party of six. The agent said we could get one room only, but Angie kept pushing and wanted to speak with a manager. The agent got a manager on the phone. Angie was aggressive and asked him, "How do you expect six people to sleep in one hotel room?" She didn't give in. Finally, the manager relented and we were booked in two rooms. This was classic Angie. She was tough when she had to be and didn't back down.

The next morning, we flew to San José but had to cancel our reservation at the Arenal rain forest hotel. That was very disappointing. After clearing passport checks and baggage claim, we piled into a private taxi and headed to our condo located near Jaco on the central coast. On our first night, we partied in an open-air bar without walls. It was fun to sip drinks and relax after all the travel nonsense. Angie loved the warm night and tropical breeze and remarked it was nice not to need a sweater.

While on the central coast, we took a snorkeling cruise, glided on zip lines through a rain forest, went deep sea fishing, and ate excellent seafood every night. The deep-sea fishing crew took us about forty miles offshore but the fishing was slow. We had to wait three hours before landing a sailfish and later caught a huge blue marlin. It was quite a sight watching the marlin jump after it was hooked. The fish was so big, we couldn't pull it into the boat. We had to photograph it pressing against the side of the hull.

We also walked the crowded streets and beaches of Jaco one afternoon and strolled across a bridge over a river teeming with crocodiles. What we enjoyed most was the closeness we experienced together as a family. The tight bond our children shared with Angie was evident on all of our Costa Rica trips. Our kids have Angie's fun sense of humor, so there always was lots of laughter and love.

There were three other Christmas trips to Costa Rica to towns in the northwestern part of the country—Tamarindo, popular with surfers, and Samara, a fishing village. We made several fun excursions on those trips. The kids took surfing lessons in Tamarindo and actually did well. We took a sailboat cruise in Tamarindo and visited a coffee plantation. We did another fishing trip closer to shore in Samara. Angie didn't want to go on this excursion, and I stayed with her. The kids caught a large mahi mahi, which we took to a restaurant in town to butcher and cut into fillets. At dinner, the mahi mahi fillets were piled high on the serving plate. There were plenty left after dinner. We ate the remaining fillets in the rental house for the rest of our stay.

Downtown Tamarindo is filled with interesting shops and restaurants. Angie and I bought flowered shirts at one store. We enjoyed dining at the beachfront restaurants with tables resting in the sand and illuminated by tiki torches. We would sit down, take off our sandals, and order a glass of wine. Tamarindo also has a large beach, on which Angie and I walked holding hands along the shore every day, letting the warm ocean water rinse our feet. Swimming in the Pacific Ocean meant floating out to an incoming wave and then letting the wave push you back to shore. I enjoyed doing that while Angie sat on the beach, reading.

Our Costa Rica vacations gave us lasting memories captured in lots of photos. Our family enjoyed strong bonding experiences during every visit to the country.

Paris

Angie and I celebrated our twenty-fifth wedding anniversary in Paris. We flew to France in late August 2009 and spent five days in the city. We stayed in a small hotel on Rue Cler, a narrow street with several outside food vendors near the Eiffel Tower. Our tiny room was on the second floor, and we could not fit in the elevator with our luggage. So we put the bags in the lift and climbed the stairs. After unpacking, we took a walk on Rue Cler and leisurely shopped for the wine and cheese we would enjoy sitting at a café table in front of our hotel. It was a great spot for people watching, seeing locals and tourists browse the shops and food stands.

After the wine and cheese snack, we walked to the River Seine and boarded a wide flatboat with rows of orange seats for an evening cruise on the river. It was a warm night. The evening views of the city were spectacular and romantic. Paris indeed deserves to be called the City of Lights. The most memorable sight was the fully lit Eiffel Tower in all its glory. After the cruise, we walked toward the hotel and stopped at a café for a late evening glass of wine. We were tired and went to bed in our cramped room about 11:00 p.m.

The next morning, I walked to a bakery on Rue Cler and picked up a baguette and two American coffees, as the locals say. Our plan that day was to first walk to the Eiffel Tower and climb the stairs to the observation deck. We waited in a long line in the hot August sun. My legs, not Angie's, were wobbly after navigating the steps to the observation deck. It was worth the effort. The panoramic view of the city was stunning.

Day two in Paris was devoted to visiting the city's iconic art museums. We picked three world famous museums: the Louvre, Musée d'Orsay, and Musée de l'Orangerie. We took the Metro to the Louvre. The subway station had stunning artwork on the walls. The Louvre is enormous and impossible to cover in one visit. The museum's paintings and sculptures span from ancient times to the nineteenth century. We, of course, were curious to see the *Mona Lisa*. We followed the signs in the gallery halls to a crowded exhibit room where the famous painting hung in a protective glass enclosure. At first, we were disappointed because we expected it to be larger. We learned that the woman shown in the *Mona Lisa* is unknown. Leonardo Da Vinci never revealed the name of his famous subject. The *Mona Lisa* once hung in Napoleon's bedroom.

Angie and I were overwhelmed by the Louvre and wandered through aimlessly. I'm not a fan of ancient art, but saw plenty of it. We stayed two hours and walked to the Impressionist art museum Musée d'Orsay. This museum is housed in a former railway station located on the left bank of the Seine. The second most visited museum in the world, it is world famous for its extensive collection of Impressionist and post-Impressionist art. We enjoyed walking though exhibits and marveled at the colorful wall-size water lily painting by Claude Monet. While there, I posed in front of my favorite Paul Cézanne painting, *The Card Players*, and Angie snapped a photo. We didn't know photography was not permitted in art museums.

The Musée de l'Orangerie, another Impressionist and post-Impressionist gallery, was our third museum of the day. It was late afternoon and we were getting tired. We didn't have much energy for this museum, so we grabbed cups of coffee in the lobby to help get an attention boost. Angie said she had seen enough artwork and would prefer to skip the Orangerie gallery. "I'm ready for a glass of wine and dinner," she said. I convinced her to hang on for a half hour, and we roamed through the museum at a quick pace.

We walked along the banks of the Seine on our way back to the hotel, and upon arrival, we stretched out in bed and dozed for an hour. Our batteries were recharged and we walked to a small bistro that had captured our attention when we walked past it earlier in the day. We relied heavily on Rick Steves's Paris guidebook for restaurant recommendations and sample walking tours. He recommended the bistro, and we were able get in, despite not having a reservation. It was a great choice. We were served by a very friendly waiter who helped us select a bottle of French white wine. Angie ordered the sea bass entrée, and I chose confit of duck. The food and wine were outstanding, and the waiter took our picture at the table. That photo is framed and now sits in a prominent spot in the lake house. I look at it every day.

The next morning, I went back to the Rue Cler bakery for a baguette and coffee, which we enjoyed in the hotel room. It was a drizzly day. Our plan was to visit the hilltop neighborhood known as Montmartre. The district is known for its scenic streets, artists painting in the public square, the Moulin Rouge nightclub, and the Sacré-Coeur Basilica on a hill overlooking the city. Vincent van Gogh and Henri deToulouse-Lautrec lived in Montmartre. Angie and I climbed the steep steps to the basilica and walked through the church, admiring the statues and artwork. We also prayed and lit candles. The view of the city from the basilica was postcard-worthy. We snapped photos of each other with the marvelous view in the background.

Angie wandered around the square, looking at paintings by the working artists. She wondered how they could earn a decent living selling their work in the square. She told me she didn't see any paintings being sold. Angie was tempted to buy some art, but didn't find a piece she liked and could hang in our home. After art shopping, we walked around Montmartre and found a café for lunch. The drizzling had stopped, so we enjoyed our lunch outside. We left Montmartre on the Metro and rode to the Les Invalides Dome to view Napoleon's tomb.

That night we had dinner at another Steves-recommended restaurant and sat at a long table with other patrons. The conversation was friendly and we talked mostly with an older couple from Florida. The husband was Swedish and belonged to the Longboat Key Golf Club in Sarasota. His wife was younger, retired, but said she formerly was active in Florida Republican politics. We showed them pictures of our kids. When we returned to our room, I lay in bed and kept asking about our dinner company. "Who is that woman?" I asked. "I've seen her on television more than once." I kept racking my brain trying to pinpoint the identity of the lady who called herself Katherine. Finally, it hit me. "She's Katherine Harris, the former Florida secretary of state and member of Congress. She became famous while presiding over the counting of disputed election ballots in the Bush-Gore election in 2000." I Googled her and the photo was a spot-on match.

On our last full day in Paris, we rode the train to Versailles and the palace of Louis XIV. The palace is an immense and opulent complex surrounded by French and English gardens. We had a guided tour through all the rooms in the palace and learned about the extravagant lives of Louis XIV and other French monarchs. Our favorite part of the tour was walking through the incredible Hall of Mirrors, with its seventeen wide mirrors and beautiful chandeliers. Room after room in the palace was elaborately decorated with period furniture and large oil portraits of French aristocrats and their wives and children. Versailles was the highlight of our Paris trip.

Paris was the perfect venue for Angie and me to commemorate our twenty-fifth anniversary. We got away from children and work and stayed focused on each other. It was a romantic renewal. The magic of this charming city inspired us to show our love in many ways—holding hands on walks, having fun conversations and laughs while sitting in cafés, or just lounging in the room and being intimate. It was obvious that Angie loved Paris and loved being with me as we enjoyed the city. Memories from that wonderful trip come back to me frequently.

Alaska

Summer 2016 marked the third year following Angie's brain cancer diagnosis. She already had endured two brain surgeries to remove glioblastoma tumors. Realizing she probably didn't have long to live, I wanted to schedule travel (while she was physically able) to some of our bucket-list destinations. At the top of that list was an Alaska cruise. We decided to parlay two destinations into one vacation. So we booked a rail trip through the Rocky Mountains on the Canadian Rocky Mountaineer railway and a cruise to Alaska on Celebrity Cruise Lines.

When researching Canadian rail trips online I was impressed with descriptions on the Rocky Mountaineer website. "A journey of incredible landscapes and endless awe in the Canadian Rockies. Meander alongside rushing rivers and past plunging gorges. Marvel at waterfalls cascading down mountainsides and sparkling glacier lakes that are so vividly blue and green that they appear otherworldly."[3] I was sold. Give that copywriter a raise.

In August, we flew from Chicago to Calgary and took a coach to the beautiful town of Banff. The scenery was spectacular. We stayed overnight in an upscale mountainside hotel and retired early.

---

3 Rocky Mountaineer (homepage), accessed March 31, 2025, www.rockymountaineer.com.

The next day we boarded the Rocky Mountaineer in Banff at 8:00 a.m. We were booked for the top-shelf Gold Leaf service. Our rail car featured domed glass perfect for viewing the majestic Rocky Mountain landscapes. The service on the train was first rate. On the sightseeing level, guides narrated what we were seeing. And there was an ongoing beverage service, which I appreciated. I enjoyed a spicy Bloody Mary for the morning ride while Angie settled for coffee. Downstairs was the dining room. All tables seated four passengers and we met and talked with some interesting folks, including a wealthy sixty-something oil executive from Texas and his wife. He told us he started as a wildcat driller and gradually built his business. His story was fascinating. He was dressed in golf attire—no Stetson hat, huge belt buckle, or cowboy boots. Breakfast featured orange or tomato juice, a delicious three-cheese omelet, a slice of multi-grain toast and a generous helping of Canadian bacon. It's hard to describe how good it was.

Back upstairs we enjoyed stunning views as the train crossed though the mountains. Speeds never exceeded 30 mph to facilitate optimal passenger viewing. Just about everyone on board was snapping cell phone pictures. Angie and I were still full from breakfast when it was time for the lunch service. Again, the food was outstanding. We enjoyed a garden salad and a salmon fillet, accompanied by steamed veggies and red mini potatoes.

Overnight, we stayed in a hotel in Kamloops in south central British Columbia. We were still full from the exquisite meals on the train and didn't bother to look for a dinner spot in town. We walked up and down the boring main street to kill time. The next morning, we boarded the train for the second leg of the trip through the Cascade Mountains ending in Vancouver. Again, the service was excellent, and breakfast and lunch were delicious. The views were not as spectacular as the Rockies but still very scenic. We arrived in Vancouver about 5:00 p.m., said goodbye to the crew members who had served us so well, and checked into the Fairmont Hotel for a one-night stay before starting the Alaska cruise.

We boarded the massive nine-deck Celebrity cruise ship at noon and had to wait with our luggage in a holding area before getting into our state room. The room was larger than expected and had a small outside balcony. We were assigned a butler, who was at our service to help with restaurant and excursion reservations, handle room service, and take cocktail orders. His name was Javier. A good friend who was an experienced Celebrity cruiser advised me to tip the butler generously at the start of the cruise to ensure excellent service. I gave Javier $50.

On the first night of the cruise we received our table reservation for all of our meals in the giant dining room. Our table was next to a window, and we had the same waiter for the entire cruise. Dinner menus were limited with usually three entrées—beef, chicken and fish. The food was decent but not outstanding. We had the top-of-the-line drink package, which covered Angie's favorite chardonnay, Ferrari Carrano, my Hendricks Gin martinis, and Maker's Mark bourbon.

Each night before dinner we had cocktails in the main bar on the fourth deck. It was quite a show watching the bartenders in action with flair, shaking, mixing, and tossing in the air martini shakers holding various cocktails. It remined me of the movie *Cocktail* starring Tom Cruise. The bar was very busy and noisy, and it was sometimes difficult to find a seat.

As we planned each day of the cruise, we decided to buy excursions for the ports at Ketchikan, Juneau, and Skagway. We allowed time each day for Angie to nap in the afternoon. She needed to rest midday to preserve her energy for the evening. The effects of two brain surgeries required that she pace herself.

In Ketchikan, we toured a scenic fishing village and watched boats float into the bay with their catches. We dropped into a nautical-and-fishing-themed bar. There were black-and-white photos on the walls showing fishermen posing with huge fish they reeled in. The bartender took a very attractive photo of Angie and me sitting at the bar. Angie flashed a warm, captivating smile. I love that picture and it sits on my coffee table.

At every port we were greeted by rows of makeshift, tacky jewelry shops, which is typical with cruise ship ports in Alaska and the Caribbean. They were eyesores polluting the shorelines.

In Juneau, Angie and I toured the beautiful Glacier Bay National Park. It was raining lightly, and fortunately we had umbrellas. We got as close to the glacier as possible and took photos. It was a terrific scene but cold and windy. The park also had a large population of colorful birds and lovely trees and flowers. We walked through most of the park and enjoyed the scenery, but I could tell Angie was getting tired.

When we returned to the ship, I asked Angie if she felt up to walking a few blocks to visit a landmark bar, the Red Dog Saloon. Angie was happy we went there. It was a true throwback— a Western, gold-rush-themed establishment with sawdust on the floor and a honky-tonk piano player. We ordered cheeseburgers and beer and returned to the ship after finishing our lunch. Angie promptly crawled into bed and fell asleep almost right away. While Angie napped, I left the ship, jumped in a cab, and visited the Alaskan Brewing Company. I took a tour of the small brewery and drank a sampler of their beers. My favorite was the Alaska White Beer, smooth and light.

Angie was awake when I returned from the brewery. We stuck to our routine of a pre-dinner cocktail at the main bar with the entertaining bartenders, followed by dinner. Alaskan salmon was on the menu, and we both ordered it. Like the other cruise ship meals, the fish was good but not great. I suppose it's hard to prepare great meals for five thousand people.

Early the next morning, I was awakened by an intercom announcement from the captain that in thirty minutes, the ship would be near the massive Hubbard Glacier. I didn't want to miss it and awoke my lovely bride from a sound sleep. She wasn't pleased, but I told her she would not want to miss seeing the glacier. It was 6:00 a.m. We dressed and ventured outside on the observation deck, but quickly jumped back inside because the weather was freezing cold. I went back to the state room and grabbed two sweaters. They helped offset the cold and allowed us to view the spectacular glacier. Huge chunks of ice kept falling into the bay, where seals swam playfully. We stayed outside for about fifteen minutes. I think Angie enjoyed seeing the glacier but maybe in her mind it wasn't worth the loss of sleep.

The gold rush town of Skagway was the final excursion port on our cruise. The highlight was a thrilling train ride sitting in a creaky old wooden rail car that might have transported gold-seeking miners to mountain streams to pan for possible treasure. The tracks curved around mountains, and we enjoyed impressive views of mountains, glaciers, gorges, and waterfalls. At the end of the line, the elevation was 2,865 feet. We walked up and down Skagway's streets and visited a gold rush museum. It was quite interesting with exhibits of old mining tools, helmets, clothes and black-and-white photos of grizzled bearded miners at work hoping for a score. The museum had a souvenir shop where I bought a t-shirt, a Skagway Alaska cap, and a shot glass. I offered to buy Angie a T-shirt, but she didn't want one. In fact, she never liked browsing through souvenir stores on trips. She called them junk shops.

Seward is where we disembarked from the ship and booked an expensive private car for the ninety-minute trip to the Anchorage airport. It was the end of a delightful ten-day vacation and our longest trip since Ireland in 1985. With no distractions from kids or work, we were free to enjoy ourselves and be reminded about our deep love for each other. We never talked about cancer, but I frequently thought about it. I'm sure her disease was on Angie's mind, too, and I think back, wondering if she feared when the tumor would reappear, force another surgery, and maybe end her life. Her courage was inspiring. She never let on that she might be dreading the future.

During our thirty-three years as man and wife, Angie and I were fortunate to travel extensively. In addition to the memorable vacations described in these pages, we also traveled to San Francisco, Napa Valley, Las Vegas, Palm Springs, San Diego, San Antonio, New Orleans, Charleston, Hilton Head, Orlando, Key West, New York, Minnesota, Colorado, London, Vienna, and Budapest. After watching photos shown on a monitor at Angie's wake, one of the mourners asked, "Did you guys ever stay home?"

Chapter 7

THIRTY-THREE YEARS OF US

Topically, this is an eclectic chapter. It doesn't follow a consistent theme, such as dating, careers, and travel. It shares stories about our personal lifestyles, everyday life routines, and highlights from key milestone events, such as wedding anniversaries. The chapter also covers trips to Napa Valley and Charleston, and an in-flight medical emergency.

Looking Good—Always

Angie was a fair skinned, beautiful Irish lady with cute freckles on her face, which emerged when exposed to sunlight. She covered them with makeup. Angie was athletic and slender and stood five feet six inches. She stayed fit and in great physical shape by working out several times a week and running. Angie was meticulous about her appearance wherever she went and always looked stylish and attractive. She was a frugal dresser who looked for bargains to add to her closet. She liked to wear scarves and owned several she wore as fashion accessories. Angie also would wear sexy red lipstick and get regular manicures and pedicures. She favored red colors for her fingers and toes.

Angie's trademark feature was her beautiful red hair, which she wore in different styles through the years. When we first met, she had permed hair styled like an Afro. I liked the look. After she started working for corporations, she wore more conservative shoulder-length, body-waved styles. She abandoned the permed style in her thirties and chose to wear her hair straight at various lengths. Sometimes she let her hair grow long to the middle of her back and, with no warning, she would cut it very short. I thought the short hairstyle was her most attractive look. Despite my frequent compliments about her short hair, she often abandoned that look in favor of longer styles. For a while, she settled on a chin-length straight bobbed style. In her fifties, she kept her hair fairly short, much to my liking.

Angie always focused on her appearance and I believe was overly concerned about her weight. She was not heavy but did gain significant weight during her pregnancies. She gained sixty pounds when expecting Margaret. After every baby was born, Angie followed an aggressive exercise regimen and her diet consisted mostly of salads. Concern about her appearance sometimes bordered on vanity. A few years after her four pregnancies, she decided she needed a facelift and tummy tuck. I argued against both procedures but she insisted she needed them. She found a highly regarded plastic surgeon, Dr. Ross, who owned a large surgical center on the near north side of Chicago.

I drove her to the one o'clock procedure and sat in the waiting room. I was told the surgeries would take about two and a half hours. So I waited and read. After three hours, I asked the nurse at the check-in desk if Angie was finished and doing okay. She made a call and learned that Angie had not yet recovered from the anesthesia and the nurse looked concerned, which made me concerned. Another half hour passed with no updates. I was starting to panic. Finally, at five o'clock, Angie was wheelchaired to the hotel room she had reserved for an overnight stay. She was in pain and was told not to sleep since she had just come out of the anesthesia. Her sister Mimi stayed with her overnight and I went home.

The next day, Angie came home with her sister and said she felt great. Her body was bruised but she was happy with the outcome.

Angie had very poor eyesight and I sometimes teased her about her Coke-bottle glasses. She had seen television commercials for an ophthalmology surgeon who performed LASIK surgery to restore 20/20 vision. The eye surgeon, Dr. Sloan, scheduled an exam and consultation with Angie and me. He said Angie was a perfect candidate for the LASIK procedure, so we scheduled it immediately. Two weeks later, I drove her to the eye surgery center, and the procedure took less than a half hour. On the ride home she cried and said she couldn't believe that her eyesight now was normal. "I'm not blind anymore," she said.

Angie's favorite garments were coats. She owned several warm woolen coats and a few stylish spring coats. She liked wearing them and would alternate her choices so she didn't wear the same coat every day in winter, as I did. Angie also owned a mink coat, which she bought at a furrier in Chicago. She wore the mink to social events at Biltmore and fit in because several other women donned minks when they came to the club. When fur became a fashion and social no-no, Angie's mink was banished to hang in an upstairs closet. She never tried to sell it. The coat is still in the closet. I have no idea what to do with it.

Our Routines

Our home life revolved around our children from 1988 to 2016. Angie's work schedule had her leaving the house about 7:00 a.m. We would roust the kids from bed at 6:00 a.m. so there would be time for breakfast. The school bus picked up the Catholic school kids quite early, and after that run, the drivers would get the public school students. Some Catholic school parents griped about the early start time, saying it wasn't healthy because their kids weren't getting enough sleep. Unlike them, Angie and I liked the early start time because we could get the kids off to school before leaving for work.

Angie normally arrived home about 5:00 p.m., but the kids would get back from school well before that. For Kathleen and Charlie, there were soccer practices a few days a week. Working at home allowed me to chauffer them to practice. If I was traveling, we would arrange with other parents to give them rides. The weekday schedule was hectic, but we made it work. Every morning, Angie assigned Michael to make her coffee and defrost a chicken or some other food for dinner that night. She paid him $25 every two weeks, a good deal for him.

Weekends generally were busy with boys and girls soccer games in the fall, basketball in the winter, and soccer again in the spring. Michael was the only kid who played baseball. On Friday nights, Angie and I would go out for dinner. Our favored places were a family-owned Italian restaurant in Palatine called Agio and the D&J Bistro in Lake Zurich. At Agio, we became friendly with the owners. The husband was a runner, so he bonded with Angie, talking about their training and races. Angie's favorite dish at Agio was saffron salmon. I liked the seafood linguine. The final time we ate at Agio was in early October 2012, a week before moving to Wisconsin. The owner sat at our table and asked, "Is this the Last Supper?"

We usually stayed home on Saturdays unless going out for dinner with friends. The routine at home was to feed the kids and put them to bed before we would make dinner for ourselves. Chardonnay was the favored beverage, of course, and we made Hunan-style dishes in our wok, following recipes in a cookbook written by the famous San Francisco chef and Hunan restaurant proprietor Henry Chung. Henry penned a note to Angie on the title page. We feasted on Hunan chicken and spicy noodles. After dinner, we watched a DVD rented from the local video store. Video streaming was not available in those days.

On Sundays we attended the 10:00 a.m. Mass at St. Theresa Church and enjoyed the coffee-and-pastry social after Mass. Our pastor was an old Irishman who had previously served at a parish near Angie's home neighborhood. He was fond of Angie as a fellow Chicago South Sider. We were active in the parish. I was president of the parish school board and, on occasion, Angie volunteered at the school helping in the library. We enjoyed our Sunday dinners at home because it was the one day we all could sit together, talk freely, and eat good food. Angie often made a tasty Italian baked chicken dish.

At least once a week, Angie and I would go out for breakfast, and we often took the kids with us. It was a ritual we followed on Saturdays or Sundays for several years. She usually ordered soft-boiled eggs. The Greek owners of two breakfast spots in Palatine knew us well.

For our entire marriage, Angie and I enjoyed conversations over glasses of wine. When Angie got home from work, after greeting the kids and asking about their days, she would open a kitchen drawer and find the corkscrew. Angie would open a bottle of Toad Hollow chardonnay, call me up from the home office, and we would sit in the sunroom and enjoy the wine and conversation for a half hour or so before making dinner. The 5:00 p.m. wine drinking became a tradition we continued as long as Angie was able. She would send me a wine glass emoji every evening to summon me from my basement office for what she called "wine time."

California chardonnay was the only wine Angie would drink and, through the years, her preferred vintages got more expensive. I tried to convince her to try some of the cabernets, merlots, and malbecs I liked, but she preferred to stick with chardonnay. When we were first married, she drank Raymond Chardonnay, which sold for under $10 a bottle. Soon she shifted to Raymond Reserve at $12.99. Raymond Reserve was Angie's chardonnay of choice for several years until she tried Toad Hollow at a wine tasting. That wine was $14.99 and became the new favorite. Angie was a Toad Hollow drinker for a about three years until we attended a house party in Inverness. The wine served was Ferrari-Carano Chardonnay. After Angie had her first glass, she was hooked and a new favorite emerged. This wine sold for $19.99. Angie's ultimate favorite chardonnay was Cakebread, but it was $50 a bottle and we bought it only for special occasions.

Hanging Out in Napa Valley

Angie and I made two trips to wine country in Napa Valley. The first was in 1993. Angie's mother watched the kids. We flew on an early evening flight from O'Hare airport to San Francisco. Our flight was delayed, and we arrived at the San Francisco airport at 10:30 p.m. The airport was abandoned, and there was only one employee at the rental car counter. We learned that the car we reserved wasn't available. The helpful desk employee felt sorry for us, so she gave us a bright red Chrysler Sebring convertible. We put the top down and drove on Highway 101 to the El Dorado Hotel in Sonoma. We breezed through the misty night for the hour-long drive to the hotel. I remember Angie's hair blowing in the wind as we went across the Golden Gate Bridge. It was a very memorable sight.

In Napa and Sonoma, we toured numerous wineries, had lunch on the Napa Wine Train, and dined at the trendy restaurant in our hotel. Despite being exposed to different varietals, red and white, at numerous tastings, Angie stuck with chardonnay. Touring the Robert Mondavi winery and riding the Sterling tram were our favorite activities during our stay. I snapped a lovely photo of Angie riding on the tram.

Our second wine country trip was in 2014 after Angie's second surgery. This time we avoided Napa because of heavy traffic on Highway 29. We stayed for four days and concentrated on Sonoma County. We hit two wineries in the mornings and two in the afternoons following a long lunch. The highlight was our visit to Angie's favorite winery, Ferrari-Carano. It was located about forty-five minutes outside Sonoma in the Dry Creek Valley. It was a huge, meticulously landscaped property with acres of beautiful gardens. Inside, the winery was lavishly decorated. There were brass handrails and foot rails on the main bar and oak was everywhere—floors, doors, tables, and bars. We tasted different vintages, including a very expensive reserve chardonnay we didn't buy. Angie was very tired after the afternoon winery tours and tastings and would nap for a couple of hours before dinner. She slept in the car on the way back from Ferrari-Carano.

Celebrating the Holidays and Anniversaries

One of my fondest memories of Angie is how much she loved Christmas. Her enthusiasm was infectious, as all of us enjoyed watching her decorate the house, wrap gifts, and get our home ready for entertaining family and friends during the holiday season. We had a garage full of Christmas decorations. She had decorations for every room in the forty-five-hundred-square- foot Inverness house, including a throwback aluminum tree, which she installed in the basement. She said that tree brought back memories of Christmastime in her childhood. I told her the tree was ugly. She just said, "I don't care. I'm keeping it."

For several Black Fridays, Angie and Marion would arrive at their meeting place at 5:00 a.m., ready to battle hordes of shoppers at Walmart, Target, and the malls. They would shop all morning and then have a leisurely lunch. Angie always returned home with bags full of gifts. She was a very organized and efficient shopper and enjoyed buying gifts for the kids.

Our family opened our gifts on Christmas morning but Angie and I opened our presents for each other on Christmas Eve after we finished putting the kids' gifts under the tree. Of course, it was tough to get the kids to go to bed, so it usually was after 10:00 p.m. before we could open wine and exchange our gifts. Our gift exchanges were romantic. We would talk about how we chose our gifts, hold each other, and kiss. Most of my presents for Angie were jewelry. Through the years, I bought her expensive necklaces, earrings, and bracelets. My gifts usually were clothes she wanted me to wear. She wasn't fond of the golf attire that was a staple of my casual wardrobe.

We celebrated our wedding anniversaries as very special occasions. Usually we would go to an expensive restaurant in Chicago, stay overnight in a hotel, and enjoy breakfast or brunch before heading home. Our milestone anniversaries were different. For our twentieth (2004) I bought Angie a compact red two-seater Mercedes hard-top convertible. I gave her a romantic card and small gift box holding the car keys. She absolutely flipped when she opened the box and saw the Mercedes logo on the key holder. We drove to the dealer to get the car. Angie put the top down and sped off for home. She loved driving that car to work every day in good weather. That vehicle did not perform well on snow and ice. Margaret also enjoyed driving the convertible.

For our twenty-fifth anniversary (2009), we went to Paris. It was my first time in the city as a vacationer, but Angie had been there on a European bus tour in her twenties. It was a romantic five days as described in Chapter Six. Our thirtieth anniversary (2014) was celebrated in Milwaukee. We stayed at the Pfister Hotel, and a bell captain with a wide handlebar mustache recommended that we have dinner at Bacchus, a local restaurant, and he made the reservation. As we drank our wine at the table before ordering entrées, a stranger came and put a large red rose on the table for Angie and said, "Happy Anniversary!" Who was it? I recognized the mustache. It was the hotel bell captain. We were impressed by his thoughtful gesture.

Amid the household commotion associated with having four active children, Angie and I found time for each other every day. In addition to our standing 5:00 p.m. wine appointment, we had breakfast alone two or three times a month, restaurant dinners on Friday nights, and relaxing time on the oversized couch in the sunroom at night. In bed, Angie sometimes would have fun role-playing. She would say, "Hey Mr. Chuck, you get in town much? Wanna have some fun?" That was her way of injecting some humor into our intimate relations. We had a fun and active sex life until cancer took away Angie's libido. But we still kissed and hugged a lot and held hands. She apologized to me for not being intimate anymore. That was a rare complaint about her illness.

After the cancer diagnosis and first surgery, I resolved that we would travel as much as possible while Angie's health allowed. The combined Canadian rail excursion and Alaska cruise was our most ambitious trip. It lasted eleven days. And one of the family Costa Rica vacations occurred after her diagnosis. Another planned Costa Rica trip had to be canceled in December 2013 because Angie was undergoing six weeks of radiation treatment in Chicago.

Low Country Cuisine and a Medical Emergency

Charleston, South Carolina was a destination neither of us had visited, and friends had told us we would enjoy visiting the city and feasting on its unique, savory cuisine. We booked a stay at the Wild Dunes beach resort located on the Isle of Palms, a barrier island thirty miles outside Charleston. We enjoyed the seemingly endless beach and took long walks. It was a relaxing stay, and the weather was excellent, with temperatures considered mild for the month of June in South Carolina. The only negative was that the restaurant in the resort was okay but not great. The menu was limited and so were the wine selections.

After three days at Wild Dunes, Angie and I hopped in the rental car and drove to Charleston. We checked into the Planters Inn, a hotel that oozed southern charm and hospitality. Our room had a king-size canopy bed and a nice view of the street. It was lunchtime, and we strolled a few blocks from the hotel and found an interesting café with a window sign boasting about their Low Country cuisine. Once seated, we ordered glasses of white wine and ordered she-crab soup and peel-and-eat shrimp. The soup was delicious, and I ordered a second cup. Angie said she would try to make it when we got home. She found a recipe and the soup she made was very good. It was close but not the same as the chowder we enjoyed in Charleston.

After lunch we headed to the Charleston City Market and filed past rows of vendors selling souvenirs, t-shirts, sandals, straw hats, and sweetgrass baskets. We bought straw hats. After we walked the entire length of the market, Angie wanted to go back to the hotel and climb in the canopy bed for a nap before dinner. We needed a reservation at the Peninsula Grill in the hotel. It was rated five stars and fully booked. I appealed to the front desk to see if we could get a table. The concierge scored a 7:30 p.m. reservation for us. The restaurant was outstanding and worthy of its five-star rating. The walls had old black-and-white photography of the Charleston seacoast and docks. We ordered the house Caesar salad, the grouper special, and chocolate-chip cheesecake for dessert. It was a memorable dinner.

Charleston is a very walkable city. After breakfast in the hotel, on our second day we walked to the seacoast and went to the end of a very long pier. We could see Fort Sumter but didn't feel like going on a tour. We also walked through the mansion district and explored one of oldest mansions in Charleston. After that, we found the Old Slave Mart Museum. It was fascinating. Charleston was a major port for the slave trade. The museum had troubling photographs and eyewitness accounts of the horror and cruelty inflicted on the Africans who were captured and shipped to Charleston.

Angie wore her straw hat to hide her very short hair that was growing out from radiation- induced baldness. We went back to our favorite café and ordered the shrimp and she-crab soup again. We couldn't resist. After lunch, we headed to King Street for some shopping. Angie wanted to look in the dress shops to get ideas for her mother-of-the-bride gown for Kathleen's wedding. She tried on three dresses in one shop, and all looked great to me. She didn't agree. She thought the dresses were too elaborate and wanted a simpler look. She bought her dress a few weeks later in Milwaukee.

Going home, we had a late morning, nonstop flight to Milwaukee's Mitchell Field airport and sat in opposite aisle seats in the middle of the cabin. About halfway to Milwaukee, Angie told me she "felt funny." Her right hand was trembling and she said she felt weak. I summoned a flight attendant who immediately asked if there was a physician on board. Fortunately, there was a doctor on the flight, an internist. He quickly examined Angie and determined that she might be on the verge of a seizure or stroke. He told the flight attendant that the plane should be diverted immediately to the nearest airport, which was Detroit. The pilot made the announcement, and the passengers near us expressed their concerns and were not upset about the diversion.

When the plane landed, a team of paramedics boarded, lifted Angie onto a gurney, and rushed her off the aircraft. She was loaded into the awaiting ambulance, which sped off to Henry Ford Hospital. I jumped into the back of the ambulance and held Angie's hand. She was conscious but disoriented. When we arrived at the hospital emergency room, the paramedics moved Angie to a bed in an examining room. She was incoherent and confused and kept saying "I have glioblastoma." Within five minutes of lying down on the bed, Angie had a massive seizure. Her head moved uncontrollably from side to side and her arms, legs, and body jerked rapidly. I was frightened and didn't know what to do. The seizure lasted about a minute and then Angie's body relaxed. She was exhausted and soon fell asleep.

The attending physician wanted to consult with the hospital's chief neurosurgeon and perform an MRI to determine the cause of the seizure. Initially, a brain bleed was suspected. I didn't authorize them to do anything. I emailed Angie's neuro-oncologist, Dr. Raizer, at Northwestern Medicine. I knew him to be very responsive to email and was confident he would answer quickly. He did and said he was on a plane waiting to take off for Los Angeles. He wrote that one of his colleagues would call me in a few minutes with instructions. Within five minutes, Dr. Raizer's colleague phoned. She first wanted to know exactly what had happened with Angie and how she was feeling.

I told her she was stable and sleeping after the seizure and related what the Henry Ford doctors had recommended. "Don't let them do anything!" she exclaimed. "Get her back here as soon as you can." She spoke to the attending physician and prescribed an anti-seizure medication. After the call, Angie was admitted and slept through the night in the hospital room, while I tried to snooze in a chair without much success.

The next morning, the chief neurosurgeon dropped in and told me I should have allowed his team to perform a scan and maybe operate. He said he strongly suspected Angie had a brain bleed. He was an arrogant prick and pissed me off with his authoritative attitude. I told him I was following directions from Angie's Northwestern doctors. He shot a dirty look at me and left.

I called Kathleen and told her about the flight diversion, seizure, and hospital stay. We needed a ride to the Milwaukee airport to fetch our luggage and drive home. Kathleen and Margaret drove to Detroit and picked us up about two o'clock. I explained everything that happened during the ride and told them how much fun we had in Charleston. Five hours later, we arrived in Milwaukee, found our luggage at baggage claim, located the car, and headed home to Whitewater. Angie slept during the entire ride from Detroit but was awake when we arrived in Milwaukee. She didn't remember anything about having a seizure and being in the hospital.

Chapter 8

BRAVING THE DARKNESS

This chapter explores our cancer saga and covers a four-year ordeal of hospitalizations, surgeries, physical therapies, and hospice care. It was October 2013 when it became evident to me that Angie was having neurological problems.

When we were constructing our new home on Whitewater Lake in 2013, we rented a house near our place from a local chiropractor. Living there for six months enabled us to check on construction progress every day. Angie was excited about the new house and loved stopping at the construction site to see what had been done every day. She would talk with the contractor, ask questions, and share her ideas about everything from bedroom sizes to outdoor lighting. This was her project. I didn't interfere because I liked most of her ideas, and it wasn't necessary for me to render opinions. But I did stay on top of the budget and watched expenses carefully. The construction loan was $650,000, which was enough to cover the building costs.

As the summer ended, Angie frequently complained about headaches and a drop foot condition that caused her to trip and fall when she climbed stairs. She also became quite forgetful. One Sunday morning, she got up early, dressed in one of her work outfits, and drove to Baxter. I thought maybe there was a meeting she had to attend, so I didn't ask why she was leaving. Angie came home about an hour later and told me she was halfway to Baxter when she realized it was

Sunday and she didn't have to be at work. That was another red flag indicating a possible neurological disorder. The other warning signs included the headache attacks, forgetfulness, drop foot, and concerns with her eyesight. She said she couldn't see very well in one eye. Angie also had a flat affect and didn't seem to care about anything. When we moved from the rental into the new house, I expected Angie to be excited. She wasn't. There were three large wardrobe moving boxes in our bedroom, and Angie didn't bother to unpack them. I did.

At the time, Angie did not have a primary care physician, but a neighbor was able to schedule an appointment for Angie with a friend who was a family physician in Lake Geneva. A physician's assistant told her the headaches were migraines and gave her a prescription for a strong analgesic. The drug helped with the headache pain but did nothing to curb the frequency of her attacks. I was becoming increasingly concerned that Angie shouldn't be driving, and I wasn't convinced she had migraines. Our daughter Kathleen and I decided Angie should see another doctor, and we scheduled her to see my internist, Lee, who knew Angie from her days working as a nurse in his practice. On October 28, Angie met Kathleen in Kenosha near I-94 and they drove to Lee's office in Highland Park, Illinois.

Lee asked Angie how she was feeling and she answered, "Fine." Kathleen interrupted fast and mentioned all the red flags we observed that could indicate a neurological problem. Lee decided an MRI exam was needed and would show if Angie had a brain tumor.

The next day, October, 29, was Angie's fifty-fifth birthday, and we drove for her MRI at a stand-alone medical imaging center in Round Lake not far from her workplace. I sat in the waiting area while she was scanned. It took about an hour. The technician gave me a compact disk with the scan image and said the radiologist's report would be sent to Lee. I talked Angie out of stopping at Baxter to work for a few hours, and we headed back to Whitewater. We were halfway home when Lee called. He told me that the radiology report identified a mass in the frontal lobe of Angie's brain. The radiologist did not say whether or not the mass was a tumor. Lee was worried and recommended we see a neurosurgeon at Northwestern Memorial Hospital, Dr. James Chandler, whom Lee knew.

When we got home, there was a voicemail from Northwestern Neurology. The caller was Dr. Chandler's nurse, Mary Ellen. She said the doctor could see us at 4:00 o'clock and for us to be sure to bring the MRI CD. It was 1:45 p.m. We hustled out of the house right away and headed to Chicago. We picked up Kathleen, who lived in Milwaukee, in Kenosha again. Fortunately, traffic wasn't bad and we pulled into the Northwester parking garage just in time for the appointment with Dr. Chandler.

Mary Ellen greeted us in the hospital lobby. She was pushing a wheelchair to take Angie up to the clinic. When we got to the examining room, Mary Ellen told us Angie would be admitted to the hospital and would be scanned again in the morning with a functional MRI. This test would better evaluate brain function and blood flow. Dr. Chandler came into the room and introduced himself. He is African American and has an impressive physique. He was friendly but businesslike. I gave him the MRI CD, and we viewed the image together. I wasn't sure if Angie was following the conversation.

Dr. Chandler pointed to a mass on the frontal lobe and said it likely was a tumor but he couldn't be sure. He said he would know more after looking at the functional MRI. After our session with Dr. Chandler, Mary Ellen took Angie's intake information and made all the arrangements for her hospital admission. She also booked a room for me at the Hyatt Hotel next to the hospital. Mary Ellen was very friendly and reassuring. She told us that Dr. Chandler was Northwestern's top neurosurgeon and had removed more than three thousand brain tumors in his career. I was impressed and relieved to learn that.

Kathleen stayed in the clinic waiting area while Angie and I met with Dr. Chandler. We did not anticipate an overnight stay and didn't pack any clothes. While I accompanied Angie to her room, Kathleen went to a Target store and bought pajamas and a bathrobe for Angie and two casual dress shirts for me. The functional MRI was scheduled for the morning, and Dr. Chandler said he would be able to share the results with us the same day. It was about noon when Chandler and two neurosurgery residents entered Angie's room. He told us the functional MRI result indicated there was a tumor in her frontal lobe, and he had scheduled her for surgery the next day, November 1. We were surprised to learn that Angie would be awake throughout the surgery, which allowed surgeons to speak with her during the procedure, make sure critical brain functions would not be compromised, and know she was able to respond to the surgeons when they spoke to her. I also was surprised that Angie's head would not be shaved. We were happy about that.

For the rest of the day, I stayed in the room with Angie, and we chatted with our kids and Angie's sisters. Angie didn't seem overly concerned about the surgery and wondered what it would be like to be awake during an operation on her brain. One of the surgical residents dropped in late in the afternoon to brief us about the surgery and predict how long it would take. After that, the kids and I went to Gino's East for deep-dish pizza and let Angie sleep and get well rested for her surgery.

The next morning, I arrived at Angie's room about 6:30 and interrupted the nurses as they were prepping her for surgery. The operation was scheduled for eight o'clock. I stood outside the room until Angie was fully prepped. I asked how she felt and she said she was nervous. I stood next to her bed and held her hand. A young orderly pushed the bed out of the room and steered it down the hallway on the way to the operating room. I walked alongside as far as the nurses would let me. I kissed my soulmate on the forehead, and my eyes welled up with tears.

The surgery is known as a craniotomy. During the procedure, part of the skull, called a bone flap, is removed temporarily to give the surgeon access to the brain. It is replaced after the procedure. The surgery is performed to excise brain tumors, relieve pressure from swelling or bleeding, repair blood vessels, and remove blood clots.

The surgical waiting room was crowded and our group included Kathleen, Charlie, Angie's sisters Mimi and Kathleen, my brother Tom, and Marion. On the wall behind the check-in desk, there was a large monitor that listed every surgical patient with the name of the surgeon and the status of the procedure, such as "In progress" or "In recovery." Angie's name was midway down the list. We chatted, drank a lot of coffee, read magazines, and paced up and down the hallway. After four hours, the scoreboard changed to read "In recovery" after Angie's name. I was called to the check-in desk and a distinguished older gentleman volunteer told me Dr. Chandler would speak to me in a few minutes.

I jumped out of my seat when I saw Dr. Chandler in his surgical scrubs approaching the waiting room. I was nervous when I greeted him. He looked at me and said, "I'm very pleased." He explained that he removed a tumor, called a glioma, from Angie's frontal lobe. The surgery was very successful, Dr. Chandler stated, because he was able to remove the entire tumor without any complications. "She should be fine," he said. I shared the good news with everyone and we waited until Angie was out of recovery and went back to her room.

As we all hugged and breathed sighs of relief, the neurosurgeon who assisted Dr. Chandler came to talk with us. He explained that gliomas are tumors that originate in glial cells in the nervous system and account for 30 percent of all brain tumors and about 80 percent of malignant brain tumors. That wasn't good news. The surgeon said the glioma removed from Angie's frontal lobe was large, about the size of a golf ball. We wouldn't know if the tumor was malignant until the biopsy was completed. He didn't know when we would know the result.

Back in Angie's room, the mood was cheerful. She was awake and seemed to be her old self again. She was talkative, and the flat affect was gone. Angie described how it felt to be awake while the surgeons were carving into her brain. She said she felt movement and pressure, and the surgeons constantly talked to her and insisted that she respond. They kept saying, "Angie how are you doing?" Angie complained that the drainage tube plugged into her head to let excess blood leak out was bothering her. She tried to pull it out, so the nurse had to tape a large mitt on her hand to keep her from grabbing the tube.

The kids left about 6:30 p.m. and Mimi stayed with me as we kept Angie company. We could see she was tiring and wouldn't stay awake much longer. I was surprised she was chatting with us so soon after surgery. I anxiously awaited news about the biopsy. My phone rang about 7:30 p.m. It was Dr. Chandler. My heart raced and my hands trembled as I anticipated bad news. Chandler told me the biopsy revealed the tumor was a glioblastoma, the most aggressive type of malignant brain tumor. He said treatment would begin soon after Angie was discharged from the hospital. He told me to contact the neuro-oncology clinic to schedule an appointment with Dr. Raizer and start therapy. Mimi saw the distressed look on my face and knew the news wasn't good. We hugged outside Angie's room, and Mimi said," We just can't catch a break." She left for home and I went to my hotel room. I hadn't eaten dinner but the uneasiness in my stomach didn't allow for much of an appetite.

When I arrived at my hotel room, I stretched out on the bed and started crying. "Dear God, why did this happen to Angie? What will we do? How long will she live?" It took several minutes for me to compose myself and stop crying. I called my brother, Tom, and shared the awful news with him. He was shocked, asked several questions I couldn't answer, and wanted to know how he could help. I said I just wanted to talk and would keep him informed about Angie's prognosis and treatments.

After the call, I started Googling on my phone to learn about glioblastoma. The lead sentence in the first article I downloaded said: "Glioblastoma is a death sentence." I wasn't sure I wanted to read further but forced myself to continue. I learned that 25 percent of glioblastoma patients survive more than a year and I thought, *Okay, Angie is very healthy so she'll live at least that long.* However, the article also reported that just five percent of patients survive more than five years, and average survival length is fourteen to sixteen months. There is no cure and therapies, if successful, can prolong life.

After reading that depressing piece, I Googled glioblastoma treatments, looking for some promising news, and numerous titles appeared on my smartphone screen. I read a few scientific articles with interesting titles until three o'clock in the morning (there was no way I could sleep). I learned that standard therapy for glioblastoma is an oral chemotherapy drug, temozolomide, and six weeks (thirty treatments) of radiation therapy. One article covered the experimental drugs in clinical trials, and immunotherapies that were cited as the most promising. This treatment targets the body's immune system to seek out cancer cells and destroy them. Even if surgery to remove a glioblastoma tumor is successful, residual cancer cells will infiltrate healthy brain tissue. This accounts for the one hundred percent recurrence rate for glioblastoma. Recurrence usually occurs within six to nine months and median survival time following recurrence is six to twelve months. One article advised that patients receive treatment at a medical center that conducted clinical trials for glioblastoma. I checked the Northwestern Medicine website and found that the neuro-oncology team was involved in several clinical trials.

The next morning, Angie was sitting up in bed and was delighted that the drainage tube in her head was removed. Her noggin was wrapped in a surgical dressing, which concealed the scar on the top half of her head. Her hair would cover it.

Mid-morning, two neurosurgeons who had assisted with Angie's surgery entered the room. Dr. Chandler was busy with surgeries that morning. They explained that her operation was successful in removing all of the malignant glioblastoma tumor. We gave our permission for Northwestern to keep the tumor for use in brain cancer research studies. Given Angie's age and excellent health, the doctors expected she would respond well to therapy, which would begin in 30 days to allow enough time for surgical healing. She would be discharged the next day.

Angie told the kids in person and on the phone the result of the biopsy and talked about the next steps in her cancer treatment. She was upbeat and said she would be fine. They knew their mother was tough and a fighter and believed her when she assured them that she would be okay.

Our first appointment at the Northwestern Medicine Neuro-Oncology Clinic was in mid-November. Dr. Raizer was the doctor in charge of Angie's care. Before seeing Dr. Raizer, Angie had an MRI to establish a baseline before therapy began. The scan was clear as expected. Dr. Raizer prescribed temozolomide, to be taken on five consecutive days at the beginning of every month, and he arranged for Angie to begin radiation treatment the following week. Angie asked about a planned Costa Rica trip between Christmas and New Year's. Raizer said we had to cancel the trip because it would interfere with the radiation schedule. We were very disappointed because the vacation was just what we needed as a family after all the stress and heartbreak of the past few months. We asked if Angie could have her radiation treatments at a radiology center near our home. He said he preferred that radiation treatments be performed at Northwestern to ensure exact adherence to the treatment protocol and make sure the radiation would be aimed at the right part of Angie's brain.

Since it would be impossible for Angie to travel five days a week from Whitewater to Chicago, we consulted with a social worker on the clinic staff to learn about housing options available to Angie. She referred us to two apartment buildings near the hospital that had agreements with Northwestern to house patients when necessary. We found a very small and reasonably priced one-room apartment with a bed, television, closet, refrigerator, and stove. The full six weeks of rent had to be paid upfront. The schedule would involve radiation on Monday afternoons so Angie could ride the train from Harvard, Illinois to Chicago in the morning. I would drive her to the train station. Radiation would be in the morning on the other days of the week, and she would take the train home on Friday mornings and get home by noon. That gave her a two-and-a-half-day weekend. On Wednesdays, I would drive to Chicago. We would go out for dinner, and I would stay overnight. Sometimes we would have breakfast the next morning before her treatment.

Angie was bored, depressed, and lonely in that tiny apartment. Her treatments were done by 9:00 a.m., except for the afternoon treatments on Mondays. For the remainder of each day, she would take long walks if it wasn't too cold, and read, or nap, or watch television in her room. We would talk on the phone every night. Our girls and her sisters visited at least once a week. Looking back, I wish I had been more aggressive in lobbying for the radiation treatments to be performed closer to our home. I don't think it would have made any difference in the outcome of the treatments. But I sided with Dr. Raizer's preference to perform the radiation at Northwestern. Angie didn't complain, but I knew being stuck in that drab apartment was a terrible experience for her.

As Angie progressed through the fourth and fifth weeks, the cumulative effect of the radiation caused significant fatigue. She needed a lot of sleep. After the fifth week, I noticed Angie was losing hair on one side of her head. She wasn't bald, but the hair was very thin. Anticipating more hair loss, we visited a high-end wigmaker in Chicago who specialized in making hairpieces for women with cancer treatment hair loss. Angie picked out a bob hairstyle wig that was close to her natural color. The stylist chopped her hair quite short so the wig would be a tight fit. When she tried on the expensive wig, she thought the hair was too long and asked the stylist to trim it. She wore the wig on the way home, but I could tell she didn't like it. When we got home, she removed it and put on a scarf. The next day she ordered a wig online and preferred wearing it instead of the custom hairpiece. Angie's hair loss worsened as we moved into the new year 2014 and she basically was bald on one side. I convinced her to let me shave the rest of her head so that her hair eventually would grow back evenly. We took a cute photo with our bald heads side by side.

Upon completion of the radiation therapy, we celebrated at our favorite local Italian restaurant, called Holi Cannoli. The radiation ordeal was over, and she was still taking temozolomide. Every three months, she would see Dr. Raizer after having an MRI. Each time Angie had an appointment with Raizer, she and I would nervously await what he would say about the scan result. If it was clear, he would put us at ease right away by saying it looked good.

In mid-February, Angie returned to work at Baxter, wearing the wig she bought online. Her colleagues welcomed her joyfully and were amazed at how good she looked and how well she functioned. She was very happy to resume her duties. For her, it was back to normal, but it was not for long.

In mid-April, the headaches were back, and so was the vision problem. I was worried about her driving back and forth to work. But she dismissed my concerns, told me not to worry, and said she could see fine with one eye. Of course, we feared tumor recurrence. We scheduled a visit with Dr. Raiser and he ordered an MRI. When he entered the exam room, he told us the scan showed a mass that could be a tumor, but he wanted Dr. Chandler to evaluate the scan. Chandler was in surgery and wouldn't be in the clinic until 1:00 at the earliest. We made an appointment for one o'clock. He would be able to read the MRI in his office. It was 11:30 a.m., so Angie and I walked across the street to Panera Bread and had lunch. We waited about twenty minutes for Chandler to arrive. He reviewed the scan on his computer and told us there was a tumor in the frontal lobe at the same location of the first tumor. Angie needed another surgery, but we could wait a week or two. We scheduled the procedure for May 8.

Angie was not visibly upset about needing another surgery and told me she recovered very well from the first operation and knew she would have another excellent recovery. Angie broke the news on the phone to our kids, her sisters, and her boss at Baxter. Margaret was the most emotional upon hearing the news, but Angie assured her the surgery would be successful and she would make a full recovery. Kathleen recalls that news about the recurrence triggered thoughts about the inevitability that her mother had a fatal disease and not much time to live.

Angie was admitted to the hospital the night before the surgery. This time she would be under anesthesia during the procedure. She was happy about that and didn't want to undergo another procedure awake. I stayed overnight at the Hyatt, and next morning on the way to Angie's room, I spotted Dr. Chandler in the lobby standing in line at Starbucks. I waited until he got his coffee before I stood in line. I didn't want to talk to him.

Angie was already prepped for surgery when I arrived at her room. We kissed. She was very upbeat and told me not to worry. Dr. Chandler stopped in to check on her but wasn't holding his Starbucks. I assumed he was a fast coffee drinker.

I sat in the surgical waiting room and was accompanied by Angie's sisters and my daughters. Three hours later, Dr. Chandler appeared and told me the surgery was successful, and he completely removed a tumor that was smaller than the first one. The biopsy would show if it was another glioblastoma.

This was a fast recurrence—just six months from the first surgery. So the temozolomide wasn't effective. I read that the survival rate following a recurrence is six to twelve months. I did not share that information with anyone.

Angie was smiling, alert, and upbeat in her room after surgery but again had to cope with the drainage tube in her head. This time she didn't try to pull it out. Dr. Chandler stopped in later in the afternoon and told Angie she could go home in two days. He said he was pleased with the surgery and advised us to make an appointment with Dr. Raizer to determine a new treatment strategy.

Angie discouraged her sisters and the kids from visiting because the surgery was successful, she felt fine, and was going home soon. It was a sunny spring day when we left the hospital. Angie slept in the car most of the way to Whitewater. It was a traffic-free ride and we were home in less than two hours. We unpacked Angie's duffel bag and opened a bottle of chardonnay, which we enjoyed on our screened back porch. She called her boss and promised she would return to work after her six-week medical leave.

The next day, we called Raizer's office and made an appointment for the following week. Angie was happy that her medical leave coincided with nice spring and early summer weather. The pier, boat lift, and pontoon boat had been installed recently and we were looking forward to cruising on the lake every day.

Dr. Raizer agreed with Dr. Chandler that Angie's second surgery was successful in removing the entire tumor, which the biopsy confirmed was glioblastoma. Raizer decided to enroll Angie in a clinical trial for an experimental drug known as ABT 414, developed by AbbVie. The drug was in early stage trials (so early that the compound hadn't been named yet) to determine its safety. The company was conducting trials to support a clinical indication and possible approval by the U.S. Food and Drug Administration for recurrent glioblastoma.

ABT 414 was a drug-antibody conjugate engineered to target a protein known as epidermal growth factor receptor (EGFR), which can fuel tumor growth. The drug delivered a toxic load inside tumor cells to stop cell division and growth. Angie had to travel to Northwestern every two weeks for drug infusions. While there, she would get eye examinations because a side effect of the drug was the development of cysts on the eyes. She used prescription eye drops to control the cysts.

Angie began the experimental therapy in June 2014. She stayed cancer-free for two years and was considered a complete responder, according to the trial protocol. Evidently, Angie's experience on ABT 414, later named Depatux-D, was not replicated enough in the trials. In 2019, AbbVie discontinued development of the drug because the studies failed to demonstrate survival benefit for subjects taking the drug compared with those given a placebo.

I was disappointed Angie wasn't allowed to remain on the AbbVie drug. It was working, but she was no longer eligible to be a trial subject, and the experimental drug could not be given to anyone outside a clinical trial. Northwestern was not involved in any other trials for recurrent glioblastoma for which Angie would be eligible. Dr. Raizer substituted a combination therapy using two chemotherapy drugs.

Following Angie's second surgery in 2014, she was determined to keep working and maintain her active lifestyle. She begrudgingly admitted that her days of running marathons were over, due to the drop foot problem. But she still wanted to jog short distances around the lake. After we finally arrived home from Charleston via Detroit, we had a next-day appointment at Northwestern with Dr. Raizer to talk about what caused the seizure and what we might be able to do to prevent another one. Before seeing the neuro-oncologist, Angie had an MRI to check for possible tumor recurrence. Dr. Raizer informed us the scan was clear, which was a relief. So a recurrent tumor didn't cause the seizure. Residual surgical trauma to her brain likely was the cause, and Angie was not taking anti-seizure medication. The doctor prescribed Kepra to prevent a future seizure.

In Wisconsin, it is illegal for anyone who has had a seizure within the last ninety days to drive a car. I informed Angie that she wouldn't be able to drive for three months. "How am I supposed to get to work if I can't drive?" she asked. So she ignored the law and drove to Baxter the following day. Fortunately, there were no more seizures until her third surgery in January 2017.

We were very fortunate that Angie's health was very good after her second brain surgery. The second half of 2014 was going to be a very busy time for us. There was the Angie's Army 10K race in mid-May, our trip to Charleston in June, Kathleen's wedding in October, and a family trip to Costa Rica in late December. She was able to participate in and enjoy all of these events.

Chapter 9

A LIGHT THAT NEVER FADES

Unbeknownst to me, 2016 would be the last happy year for us. Angie was remarkably active going to work every day and looking forward to the trips we had planned: Napa Valley wine country, the train ride through the Rockies, and the Alaska cruise. We also booked a January 2017 vacation in St. Lucia.

In March, I became increasingly aware that Angie should not be working full time, or at all. I worried about her one-eyed driving an hour each way to Baxter in Round Lake. She told me she took long naps in the office inside her employee health clinic. Her administrative assistant covered for her if Angie's phone rang or someone wanted to see her. I couldn't believe Angie was getting away with napping on the job, and begged her to take permanent disability and earn 50 percent of her salary, which would be about $35,000. She fought me on that and insisted she was fine and fully capable of working full time.

Angie's Baxter friend Peg said she observed a noticeable decline in Angie's performance after the second surgery. There were some record keeping problems Angie was blamed for and she apparently mishandled one or more employee flu shots. Her boss confronted her, and Angie angrily defended herself. The argument was heated. Management believed Angie's medical issues posed a risk to employee health and safety if she continued in her nursing job. She was laid off and offered a paltry severance of $12,000, provided she sign a waiver to prevent her from pursuing legal action against Baxter. In essence, she was getting $1,200 for each of her ten years of service.

Angie called from her car on the way home to tell me she had been laid off. I was outraged at how poorly she was treated. Instead of firing her, why not grant this loyal employee long-term disability compensation? I called an attorney friend and asked what we should do. He said he couldn't advise me because Baxter was a client of his law firm. But he did recommend a lawyer who represented unfairly discharged employees. "I've been crossing swords with him for many years. He's the guy you need."

Angie and I sat in the kitchen and called the recommended lawyer. We explained the situation, and right away he told Angie not to sign the waiver. Then he asked what I asked: "Why didn't they put her on long-term disability?" He said he knew a lawyer at Baxter and would call him in the morning. He called us the following afternoon and said Baxter had agreed to long-term disability. We had to apply at the human resources office in Round Lake and also apply for Social Security disability. The combination of the Social Security benefit and the Baxter disability pay was supposed to equal 50 percent of Angie's salary. And it did. We considered it Angie's retirement pay. She collected for the rest of her life.

May 2016 marked the first time Angie did not have a job since the age of sixteen. She passed the time watching movies on Netflix and cruising with me on the pontoon. Sometimes she would visit her sisters. Although her marathon-running days were over, she was able to run a couple of miles and did so a few times a week. She was frustrated that she couldn't follow her previous training regimen.

Kathleen was employed at Rockwell International in Milwaukee. She was working in procurement and supply chain management. In 2015, a colleague showed her a job posting and told her he'd apply if his wife wasn't eight-months pregnant. The job was in Chicago and the employer was the Chicago Cubs. She jumped on it and snagged an interview. Her first meeting was with the chief financial officer, who was a fellow Marquette alum. Naturally, their chemistry was very good, and Kathleen breezed through two more interviews. She was hired and moved to Chicago.

In 2016, the Chicago Cubs won the World Series. Kathleen and Paul attended every World Series game in Chicago and Cleveland, and she was given a huge, jeweled ring, similar to the ring the players received. As a lifelong suffering Cubs fan, for me this was a dream come true. It was so much fun for me to witness the excitement Kathleen experienced. The Cubs dominated the year 2016 for our family, but during Thanksgiving week, after the Cubs hysteria had died down, we all got together for fun and sun in Key West. Our kids preferred to vacation during Thanksgiving week because they only had to take three days off work for a weeklong vacation.

Kathleen rented a large condo about a half mile from Duval Street, which is the main shopping and entertainment venue in Key West. We enjoyed all four days of our stay, exploring various points of interest and popping in and out of shops, bars, and restaurants. We walked all over Key West. The highlights for me were the Ernest Hemmingway Home and Museum, the Harry Truman Little White House museum, and Sloppy Joe's, the iconic Key West watering hole made famous by Hemingway. The walls in the bar are adorned with large black-and-white photos of the famous novelist posing next to huge sailfish he had hooked and reeled in. I bought a T-shirt that had Hemingway's face on the back.

We also took a snorkeling cruise in the Gulf of Mexico. The kids enjoyed snorkeling and kept at it for about an hour, but Angie preferred to remain on the boat and I stayed with her. We both sipped tropical cocktails.

Key West is well known for its beautiful sunsets. Every day of the vacation at about 4:30 p.m., we went to a bar with a nice balcony overlooking Mallory Square, which is considered the top site for viewing sunsets. We weren't disappointed. Our son-in-law Paul ordered bottles of chardonnay for our sunset viewings. The sun lowers fast on the horizon in Key West, and Mallory Square was dark at 5:30. After finishing the wine, we headed back to Duval Street to find a restaurant for dinner.

Angie tired easily on this trip. She would go with us in the morning for breakfast (her favorite meal) and join everyone for walks on Duval Street and in other parts of town. By noon, she was too tired to continue walking and sightseeing. I went with her to the condo because I wasn't sure she could find her way there alone. She always would apologize for leaving us, but I assured her that we all understood why. The damage to Angie's frontal lobe caused by the brain tumor was responsible for the behavior changes we all noticed following her second surgery.

The frontal lobe is the part of the human brain that regulates several high-level brain functions. It is located behind the forehead and governs executive functions, such as planning, decision-making, problem-solving, and judgment. The frontal lobe also influences emotions and short- term memory. In Angie's case, we noticed that her emotions became suppressed, she had a limited attention span, and her short-term memory was impaired. On a Friday night after we returned from Key West, Angie and I had appetizers and drinks at the bar in our local Italian restaurant. A couple we knew, who had an impressive house across the lake, approached us to say hello. We talked briefly. After they left, Angie said she didn't know them. I was surprised she said that because we recently had been to the couple's home for a party.

In what would turn out to be our last vacation together, in mid-January, 2017, Angie and I traveled to a beautiful Caribbean island,

Saint Lucia. We stayed at a high-end, all-inclusive resort, the Hideaway at Royalton St. Lucia. It was located on an expansive beach, perfect for walking. On the way in from the airport, we saw numerous banana plantations with bunches hanging from tall plants and wrapped in protective plastic coverings. The hotel had a comfortable open-air lobby and dining area. The beach had plenty of comfortable lounge chairs. Our routine in Saint Lucia was very laid-back. Angie didn't feel well and had limited energy, and the headaches were coming back.

We ate all our meals in the resort. Breakfast and lunch were served buffet style, and dinner had table service. We took two excursions—a trip to the main shopping area in the Castries Market and a private car tour of the entire island. The shopping area was crowded and had an unpleasant smell. We didn't buy anything. For the private car tour, our driver was a native Saint Lucian named Guy. In three hours, we rode around the island and saw glorious seaside views: the island's famous twin peaks Gros Piton and Petit Piton, beaches with dark volcanic sand, and Sulphur Springs, where you can take a mud bath or soak in mineral-rich hot springs. We skipped the mud baths.

Our days in Saint Lucia were spent reading and walking on the beach. The weather was spectacular. I was very concerned about Angie's headaches, because she was telling me they were getting worse and the best non-prescription analgesic we could find at the resort was Tylenol Extra Strength. I feared the increasingly intense headaches were a harbinger of tumor recurrence. The headaches were not constant, however. They came as attacks lasting several minutes.

An appointment for an MRI and a meeting with Dr. Raizer were scheduled for the last week in January. Angie was hurting and spent most of her time at home after returning from St. Lucia, sleeping or watching movies. But we still had our standard five o'clock wine appointment.

At every one-year anniversary of Angie's diagnosis, we would drink a toast to another recurrence-free year, like 2015. I told Angie we were signing one-year contracts with God every year to stay tumor-free. I likened it to the arrangement the Los Angeles Dodgers had with their longtime manager Walter Alston. He managed the Dodgers for seventeen years on consecutive one-year contracts. I thought the analogy was appropriate, but Angie said it was stupid.

The MRI in late January confirmed my suspicion—and I think Angie's—that her headaches were caused by another frontal lobe tumor. Her third surgery was scheduled for January 31. I asked Dr. Chandler how his patients had responded after multiple surgeries. He told me he had several who had undergone three or more surgeries. Many of them, he said, had responded very well and were fortunate that their recurring tumors could be removed surgically without complications. Chandler said he expected that a patient in excellent health like Angie would respond to a third brain surgery as well as she did after the first two surgeries.

For the third time in four years, I walked alongside the gurney transporting Angie to the surgical suite. I squeezed her hand, placed my other hand on her forehead, and said, "I love you sweetheart." She smiled and whispered, "I love you, too." Tears rolled down my cheeks as I found my way to the surgery waiting room. I checked in with the same dapper elderly volunteer as I did for the second surgery. He wore a navy-blue suit, white shirt, and a blue polka-dot bow tie. He was the best-dressed man in the room. And you could tell he was very conscientious about his volunteer duty.

Our waiting room crew this time was Kathleen, Margaret, Mimi, Marion and my brother Tom. After three hours, the dapper gent at the check-in desk summoned me and said Dr. Chandler would be available in about fifteen minutes. As the surgeon approached, the look on his face conveyed bad news. During the surgery, Angie had a massive seizure and was comatose. Chandler said seizures always were a risk in brain surgeries, but Angie's was so severe that it induced a coma. He would not speculate on how long Angie would lie in the coma.

We waited in Angie's room in the intensive care unit for the nurses to wheel in Angie's bed. She was motionless and the nurses proceeded to adjust the IV lines in her arm, place electrodes on her head to monitor her brain function, and accommodate the ventilator installed during surgery to take care of her breathing. I couldn't believe what I was seeing and feeling. Sadness permeated the room. There was the love of my life, lying helpless and motionless while being kept alive on a ventilator. As I watched the ventilator help Angie breathe, I honestly believed it was the end of the line for us. The neurologists attending to Angie would not say when or even if she would wake up. And if that wasn't enough bad news, the electrodes on her head were transmitting signals from her brain, showing she was still having seizures, even though there were no visible symptoms. She would stay in intensive care as long as seizures were detected.

I was devastated and prepared myself for Angie to die any day. But I kept thinking about the toughness and determination that enabled her to overcome many obstacles and challenges she encountered in her life. *Yeah. She will beat this and sit up in the bed and ask what all of us were worried about.* I wondered what was going on in her brain. Was she subconsciously thinking about anything? One of the neurologists provided some encouragement. She said the monitor showing Angie's brain activity was showing that the seizure activity was slowing. The neurologist surmised that Angie might wake up from the coma when the seizures stopped. She offered no guarantees but said it was possible.

Too many of us were hanging around in Angie's ICU room. The hospital's rules allowed only two family members to be in the ICU at one time. The nurses were patient and politely requested that we obey the ICU rules. We didn't argue and took turns staying with Angie. Mimi is a former cardiac ICU nurse and she maintained good relations with ICU nurses on every shift. In a stroke of genius, she ordered pizzas for the nurses on the late shift. And she made food orders for nurses on other shifts. As a result of Mimi's thoughtfulness, the nurses on every shift ignored the rule when we over-populated the ICU room. They would walk by and smile at us.

After two days, there was a breakthrough. First, Drs. Chandler and Raizer visited Angie and told us they were confident she would come out of her coma. Chandler said he had successfully removed Angie's third glioblastoma tumor. I silently took issue with his use of the word successfully since Angie had come out of surgery in a coma.

Mimi got excited that day when Angie squeezed her hand. This was Angie's first physical motion since the surgery. The same day, doctors took her off the ventilator because she was able to breathe normally, and the brain function monitor was showing that seizure activity was barely negligible.

"Way to go, Ang!" I exclaimed. "You are fighting back like you always do." *Just another obstacle for her to overcome,* I thought. The next day, a neurologist removed the electrodes from Angie's head. The seizure activity had stopped. Mimi was moving Angie's legs back and forth to help keep her muscles strong, and she showed Kathleen and Margaret the technique, which they performed properly.

Each day, Angie made remarkable improvements. She had progressed a long way from being comatose a couple of weeks earlier. She was moving her limbs, verbalizing, and sitting up in bed. She wasn't eating or drinking much on her own because it was difficult for her to swallow. She was moved out of intensive care and into a standard hospital room. Now that the intensive care phase was over, it was time to start considering rehabilitation options because she wouldn't be able stay in the hospital much longer.

Rehabilitation

I was sitting in Angie's new room when a physician assistant on Dr. Chandler's team visited to talk about moving Angie to an inpatient sub-acute physical rehabilitation facility. Sub-acute rehab provides less intense therapy than acute rehab, and patients usually receive therapy for about two hours a day. Angie's weakened physical condition called for her to move into sub-acute rehab. So my job was to quickly find a facility for Angie, but I knew nothing about physical rehab or how to go about finding a facility appropriate for her.

A friend of Kathleen's from high school worked as a manager in a physical rehab hospital. She informed Kathleen about a highly rated sub-acute faczility in west suburban Downers Grove, called Providence Rehabilitation. I scheduled an appointment with the facility administrator and got a tour of the facility. Providence basically was a nursing home with its own medical staff and physical therapists. It had a large gym where Angie's rehab sessions would take place. The administrator told me there was a vacancy for Angie and she could move in upon discharge from Northwestern.

Angie had a simple private room at Providence, and the nursing staff was very attentive. The nurses' station was directly across from her room. Our family developed a visitation strategy so Angie would never be alone. The team of regular visitors would be my kids Kathleen, Charlie, and Margaret; Angie's siblings John, Mimi, Michael, and Kathleen; and her good friends Colleen and Marion. Since Providence was two hours from Whitewater, I would visit on Mondays, Wednesdays, and Fridays, and my kids would be there on weekends. The others would come at their convenience. Mimi, Kathleen, and John visited several times a week.

We kept a journal in which everyone would summarize their visits and express current thoughts. The love for and devotion to Angie shown by everyone was inspiring. They put aside their lives and made personal sacrifices to be with Angie and care for her. They would help her with meals, even if she didn't want to eat; her sisters and Colleen and Marion made sure her hair looked good and her nails were trimmed and polished. Everyone would wheel her outside, weather permitting, to sit in the sun. The journal offered an excellent account of her treatments and the progress she made.

Angie's daily routine at Providence was breakfast followed by a physical therapy session. The therapy made her very tired, and she would nap after the morning sessions. Whoever was visiting would try to get her to eat some lunch and have enough energy for her afternoon therapy. After that session, the day was done, and she would enjoy the company of her visitors, maybe eat something on her dinner tray, and watch television. Bedtime usually was never later than 8:00 p.m.

Angie slept most of the day when not in therapy during her first two weeks at Providence, but her sister Kathleen would try to stimulate her. As she wrote in the journal on March 9: "I did some work with her on the iPad going over some words. I tried to get her to use her finger to get the word into the right box. She can't do it on her own, so I have to bring her finger to the screen. I think it stimulates her a little."

Colleen recorded some improvement on March 21: "Angie was quite talkative, if not using the right words, but much more expression in her speech. We went for a stroll outside."

On April 3, Kathleen expressed some optimism about the progress of therapy. "At PT she walked 80 feet, then more. She is hunched over like the Hunchback of Notre Dame. I'd like to sit her on the edge of the bed and practice sitting up. It might translate into walking straight up. This is the first time I saw her walk. She is progressing but requires a lot of coaxing."

A day later, her brother John expressed concern that Angie was refusing to eat: "Angie is just not hungry. It seems progress has slowed."

On April 7, Angie was promoted for acute physical rehab and moved to the Marianjoy Rehabilitation Hospital in Wheaton, Illinois. Mimi wrote: "Well here we are. A lot to get used to and everyone is very nice."

On April 24, I wrote: "She's very alert! Did well in speech therapy but hated the recreational therapy. Therapist tried to get her to do a cat puzzle. No way! Played music in her room. She knows the lyrics for Billy Joel and 'My Girl.' Walked about 90 feet in PT with lots of help. She's drinking more water."

Her sister and brother and my kids started bringing food from McDonald's. Kathleen (sister) wrote on April 30: "Brought a small order of fries and a frappé from McDonald's. She ate all of the fries and drank a little of the frappé."

Comments from all her visitors stressed that Angie always seemed very tired. This wasn't surprising because the more intensive therapy provided in acute rehab caused Angie to tire easily. Angie's stay at Marianjoy was subject to weekly evaluations to determine if she was making enough progress to justify keeping her at the facility. So I had meetings every Friday with Angie's case manager, an attractive and friendly young black woman. She would review the evaluations from Angie's therapists and determine if Angie was showing enough progress to warrant continuation of her stay. When she passed the evaluations, the case manager would authorize another week of therapy for Angie's health insurance coverage. Every week, I felt pressure about what the evaluations would recommend. The case manager assured me that Angie's week-to-week progress was tracking well, but I was nervous during every Friday review meeting.

I visited Angie at both rehab facilities on Mondays, Wednesdays, and Fridays. I always would watch her rehab sessions and talk to the therapists, who seemed to like Angie. They cheered for her during rehab. I usually talked with one or more therapists to learn how they were evaluating Angie's progress. I was very impressed with their dedication and honesty. When the morning sessions ended, I was back in Angie's room with her and would try to engage her in conversation with mixed results. If she was alert and not wanting to sleep, I would get coffee and she would take a few sips. I would talk to her about the news, our dogs, and the kids. Quite often, her sisters Mimi and Kathleen would be visiting, too. Angie was never alone. I believed she was able to follow conversations and sometimes contribute. She could answer questions capably, but when she tried to initiate talk, her speech was unintelligible. I tried to convince myself that our relationship was normalizing and was encouraged when Angie was alert and talking. But I knew better. I realized that Angie had made excellent progress after awaking from her coma, but I was afraid she wasn't going to improve much more after three months had passed. I knew the woman of my dreams was irreparably impaired, and all I could do was adjust and pray for her.

Going Home

Toward the end of May, Angie's evaluations were not showing sufficient progress required to stay at Marianjoy. She was not doing well when they shifted her to more strenuous and difficult therapies. The case manager on Friday, May 23, told me Angie would not be approved for further therapy at Marianjoy. She contacted Providence and learned that a room would be reserved for Angie, if we requested. I wasn't sure what to do until the family was able to meet and discuss our options. Her sister Kathleen asked me if I was thinking about bringing Angie home and exploring local home health care and home physical therapy resources. I told her I was leaning that way because I didn't think going back to Providence would be best for Angie. I consulted with the kids and they agreed it was time for Angie to come home.

Before Angie moved home, she had a doctor's appointment and an MRI at Northwestern. We learned that Dr. Raizer was no longer seeing patients. We decided to switch from the Northwestern's downtown campus to its newly acquired oncology center in Winfield. It was a two-hour drive from Whitewater, and I didn't have to deal with Chicago traffic and expensive downtown parking. Her neuro-oncologist there would be Dr. Grimm. He switched Angie's treatment to Avastin, a biologic anti-cancer drug that restricts the blood supply fueling tumor growth. Angie would go to the Winfield cancer center every two weeks for infusions of Avastin.

From her podiatry practice, Kathleen had extensive contacts with home health providers. She knew a woman whose company placed live-in caregivers, which is what we would need to care properly for Angie at home. Kathleen learned that an experienced caregiver with excellent references was available and looking for a placement. Her name was Natasha and she was from Ukraine. We arranged a meeting with her on Saturday in Angie's room at Marianjoy. We liked her and talked about her experience and what her duties would be with us. She would live in the lake house and be available twenty-four seven to care for Angie. She had a car, which was a plus. We hired her for $5,000 a month, of which a flat ten percent fee was paid to the placement agency. Insurance would not cover this cost, so we allocated all of Angie's disability income to pay for most of the monthly fee.

We brought Angie home on Sunday, May 25, which was Memorial Day weekend. Natasha followed us all the way to Whitewater. Charlie rode with her to make sure she didn't get lost. We didn't have an entrance ramp at the front door and Charlie and I had to carry Angie into the house and place her in the portable wheelchair I bought at a local medical supply store. I also purchased a manual Hoyer lift to maneuver Angie in and out of bed.

Natasha was a hard worker and never took days off, even though I encouraged her to get away whenever she wanted and maybe visit her sister in Chicago. Nope. She insisted on caring for Angie seven days a week. Natasha slept in the small bedroom upstairs and had plenty of space for her clothes. She prepared our meals, cleaned the house, and took excellent care of Angie. She changed Angie's diapers, dressed her every morning, made sure there would be no risk of bed sores, and she patiently helped Angie eat her meals. Most of the time it took an hour or longer for Angie to finish eating.

A hockey fan, Natasha would watch Chicago Blackhawks games with me after we put Angie in bed. She knew the Russian players on the team. Natasha usually went to bed at 9:00 p.m. and she would check on Angie at 2:00 a.m. She was an outstanding, hard-working caregiver. I felt very fortunate to have her.

Natasha's elderly mother and father lived in Ukraine and her son was an officer in the Russian army and claimed to be close to Vladimir Putin. Today, I wonder if Natasha's family survived the Russian invasion and devastation of her home country. Every week, Natasha would call her parents using prepaid phone cards on our landline. She never was able to get service on her cell phone.

Angie's routine at home was to be lifted out of her bed around eight o'clock in the morning and into the portable wheelchair to move to the dining table for breakfast. She would eat scrambled eggs and drink some coffee. During the day, Angie would participate in physical, occupational, and speech therapy sessions provided by staff from Aurora Home Health Care. The physical therapist focused on assisted walking, the occupational therapist would help Angie with her hand movements, and the speech therapist would ask Angie to identify people in our photo albums. Mimi and Colleen would visit at least once a week and our kids would come on weekends. In the late afternoons, Angie, Natasha, and I would sit on the screened porch and enjoy a glass of wine before dinner. Angie would look out at the lake and I would try to keep her engaged by asking questions. After Natasha fed Angie her dinner, we would lift her onto the recliner in the family room to watch television. She liked to watch *Law and Order*.

When Angie started falling asleep in the chair, Natasha and I would move her into the wheelchair and get her ready for bed. Natasha would wash her face and brush her teeth, and I would sit next to the bed and hold Angie's hand until she fell asleep. We were able to bring Angie into the bathroom shower next to the bedroom three times a week.

Every two weeks, Angie and I would drive to the Northwestern Cancer Center in Winfield. There was a very helpful parking attendant at the center and he would help me get Angie out of the car and into a wheelchair. He told me that he was a hockey goalie on his club team. We chatted about hockey and I told him my son Michael played for his high school hockey team. Before Angie would get the Avastin infusion, the nurses weighed her in the wheelchair and took her vital signs. The infusion would take about an hour. The nurse had to wear a protective gown and mask while she prepared the intravenous line to administer the biologic drug. Avastin had special handling instructions to prevent contamination and infection. It always was difficult to start the IV because the nurses had trouble finding a vein. After the infusion, we would drive back to Whitewater. Natasha would meet the car, and we would lift Angie into her wheelchair and push her up our newly installed ramp into the house.

In September, the physical therapy team told me that Angie was regressing and that further sessions probably would not be worthwhile. I also noticed that she was sleeping much more and sometimes would not want to get out of bed. Her next appointment at the cancer center was in early October. Angie was scheduled for an MRI and a visit with Dr. Grimm in addition to the Avastin infusion. Mimi came with me for this appointment.

Dr. Grimm was tall and very slender. He carried an old-fashioned black doctor bag. Grimm asked Angie how she was feeling. She answered, "I'm fine." The MRI scan was loaded onto the desktop computer in the examining room. The doctor opened the file and we looked at the image. He said that Angie's brain had changed a lot since her last scan. Pointing to the area around Angie's brain, he said the white matter was deteriorating and there was no way to treat or prevent it.

White matter surrounds the brain and regulates communication between different regions of the brain and spinal cord. When it deteriorates, it can impair the patient's ability to communicate and function.

Grimm said the condition was caused by all the radiation Angie was exposed to in her first round of treatment. "We don't see this very often because most of our patients don't live long enough for this to occur," Grimm explained. So Angie's glioblastoma longevity ultimately would be her downfall.

We asked Dr. Grimm if we should continue with Avastin. He said no. The white matter deterioration made further cancer treatment meaningless. He suggested we start hospice. Angie was unaware of what we learned and just sat with us, not knowing that we decided to discontinue treatment and let her die. On the way home, a nurse from the cancer center called and expressed her sympathy, but said she was proud of me for making the right but very difficult decision. I didn't expect that call but thanked her for thinking about me.

The next day, the Aurora Hospice people came to the house and delivered a new hospital bed and a high-back wheelchair. Part of hospice-at-home service was a weekly visit from a hospice nurse to examine Angie and think ahead regarding when she most likely would die. The white matter deterioration severely impaired Angie's brain function. She slept almost constantly and could hardly talk. Communication was difficult, but at times I could solicit yes-or-no answers to simple questions. All I could do was sit next to the bed and hold her hand. We fed Angie through the feeding tube in her stomach and put ice chips in her mouth to prevent excessive dryness.

I told the kids in separate phone calls what we learned about the white-matter deterioration and my decision to discontinue cancer treatment and start hospice. They were sad but understood and did not second-guess my decision, which we all believed was inevitable.

Every night I would sit next to Angie in her hospital bed as she slept. She was not in a coma but I never knew if she could hear me talking to her. I think she liked hearing the light rock music we played constantly in her room.

At two o'clock in the morning on January 9, 2018, Natasha knocked on my bedroom door, and she didn't need to say anything. The look on her face said it all. Angie had passed away in her sleep. I dressed quickly and went to see her. She was lying peacefully. Her eyes and mouth were closed. I placed my hand on her forehead. She was still warm and probably was dead for less than an hour. There was no death smell in the room. I kissed her forehead, said a prayer, and had a mental visualization of a lovely bride walking arm-in-arm with her dad joyfully anticipating her new life as my wife. She was fifty-nine and we were married for thirty-three years and four months. The cause of death listed on the death certificate is glioblastoma.

I spent about ten minutes alone with Angie and left the room to call the hospice nurse. She rang the doorbell fifteen minutes later. She had visited Angie three days ago and told me she thought the patient would live another two or three weeks. The hospice nurse handled all the death details. There was no need to contact the police or county coroner, and someone from the local funeral home was on his way to collect the body. We had arranged for Angie's wake and funeral to be held in Illinois at Davenport Family Funeral Home in Lake Zurich and St. Theresa Catholic Church in Palatine, our home parish for many years. The nurse handled the paperwork required for the local mortuary to transfer Angie across the state line.

The funeral home worker arrived carrying a body bag. I could not bring myself to watch him remove Angie from our house. I walked away from the room. After Angie's body was taken away, I walked back into her room and found a long-stemmed red rose on the pillow. My next task was to give the bad news to our children and Angie's sisters.

Natasha was sitting in the family room holding a long and very thin lighted candle. She said lighting the candle is a Ukrainian tradition to commemorate a loved one's death. Natasha's service was over, but I told her she could stay with us as long as needed. The next day she drove to Chicago to stay with her sister and look for a new job placement.

Chapter 10

MEMORIES SHARED, LIVES TOUCHED

For this memoir I'm including comments, recollections, and reflections about Angie and her life from family members and close friends. Their insights about her offer unique perspectives about Angie as a mother, sibling, colleague, and trusted friend.

Kathleen

Let's start with our oldest child, Kathleen. She is thirty-seven years old. She married Paul in 2014, and has three children: Rosemary, six; Michael, four; and Margo, two. The family lives in Chicago on the city's North Side in the Roscoe Village neighborhood. Kathleen works at Great Wolf Lodge and is responsible for purchasing and procurement for the company's nationwide water park resort facilities.

When asked by me to talk about her mother's finest personal qualities, Kathleen said her mother never stayed mad too long and usually was fun to be around. "You always knew where you stood with her. There was no guessing or walking on eggshells. She held you accountable for your behavior. She would address a problem with you and move on," Kathleen recalled. She noted that the family always spent time together in the family room and didn't separate themselves. "She instilled that inclusiveness culture in our family and she dominated the household. Dad was quieter and more laid-back, which brought good balance to their marriage."

Kathleen noted that her perspective as the oldest in the family probably offers a different viewpoint from her siblings. She said she admired Angie's inclusive personality and that she was never too busy to talk with or help her. "She was remarkable at balancing her time for family, job and, for a while, school. She had a very high energy level," Kathleen added.

"And Mom had this confidence about her; she liked what she liked. It is something I hope to instill in my own children."

As a parent herself, Kathleen says she takes after her mother in some of her mannerisms and self-deprecating sense of humor. "I hear her when I yell at my kids. I say, 'You guys are being too giddy' and that's exactly, word for word, what Mom would say to us. She was the master at being there but not doing things for you. Mom was able to be supportive, but also instilled a sense of independence in each of us. I never wanted her to do things for me, I just wanted her to be around as I did them."

Kathleen has fond memories of running marathons with her mother. They ran together in the Milwaukee Marathon in October 2011 and in the Ice Age Trail 50K run through the Kettle Morriane Forest. The Ice Age Trail race was Angie's idea, and it was her final marathon race.

"We were overconfident about what we could do on the Ice Age Trail. But we had never run in a trail race. It was a rugged experience tramping through the woods on uneven ground. But we finished the race." Kathleen remembers that Angie was always pushing herself to do more. "She had a competitiveness that would come out. It wasn't a competition that you could always see; it was more internal. She would push herself to do things. It would sometimes be a one-way competition no one knew anything about."

After that marathon, Angie complained her foot was bothering her. She blamed the difficulty of running on the uneven terrain as the cause. She was wrong. The problem was a condition known as drop foot, and it often is caused by nerve or neurological damage that makes it difficult to lift the front part of the foot. Soon after that race, I noticed that Angie had trouble climbing stairs and fell a few times.

Kathleen was the first in the family who became aware that Angie was experiencing neurological difficulties besides drop foot. "You could tell something was very off with her. She had trouble maintaining a conversation, complained of bad headaches, could be relatively disoriented, and even would randomly sing," Kathleen said. "One day she put a full cup of coffee in her purse. Her increasingly bizarre behavior led me to insist that she see a doctor. An MRI showed she had a brain tumor."

Paul, Kathleen's husband, remembers that Angie made you free to be yourself. "My best memories are when we could just hang out with her at the lake. She was fun to be with."

Kathleen also noted that Angie taught Paul how to hug.

Charlie

Our oldest son Charlie is thirty-six years old and lives in Snohomish, Washington with his wife Kelsey and their baby son Miles. They married in 2021. Both Charlie and Kelsey work at home for information technology companies.

"She was a great mom who knew what was right for you even if you didn't agree." That sums up how Charlie remembers Angie. "She could be stern, held us accountable, and gave us freedom, which we never abused. We knew what we had to do to make her happy."

Charlie considers Angie's best quality to be her strong determination to be the best she could be at whatever she endeavored. "She was always looking to improve, whether it was competing in marathon races or working as an occupational health nurse at Baxter."

According to Charlie, Angie always was upbeat and hated complainers. "She never complained during her ordeal with brain cancer," he recalled.

Angie liked to have a good time, Charlie said, and the kids enjoyed and valued the times when Angie became "Vacation Mom." That role meant she didn't have to act like a parent. Vacation Mom usually surfaced on weekends at the lake. "It was always a good time at Whitewater because she acted happy-go-lucky and wasn't worried about anything. With her, it was all about having fun together as a family."

Charlie recalls when Angie worked for the Hoveround Company selling motorized wheelchairs and the kids would beg her to let them race the wheelchairs down the driveway to get the mail. "She finally relented and we had a blast flying down our driveway and into the street."

Asked what traits he inherited from his mother, Charlie said they are caring about others and stubborn. "When Mom decided she wanted to accomplish something, she wouldn't let anything stand in her way. She wanted to get certified as a personal trainer and made it happen. She wanted to run marathons and competed in and crossed the finish line in eleven races. She wanted to earn a master's degree in nursing and did it. I learned from her. When I set a goal, I work like hell to achieve it."

Kelsey recalls asking Angie how she enjoyed the Canadian Railway Rocky Mountain tour and the Alaska cruise. She said Angie beamed and told her about meeting HGTV's Property Brothers on the train. Forget the stunning scenery, forget the delicious meals, the highlight of the trip for Angie was meeting the stars of an HGTV show. I took a photo of her smiling with the Property Brothers.

"The Webers were a treat for me," said Kelsey. "When Angie wanted to have fun, we all joined in. I was impressed with how she fostered a very close family dynamic."

Margaret

Our daughter Margaret is thirty-three. She married Matt in 2020, and has two children: Scott, two, and Bridget, one. She lives in Chicago's Logan Square neighborhood, and has worked for a digital marketing consulting firm for seven years.

Margaret's first comment to me about Angie was, "She knew what hat to wear at the right moment. She knew when to be our parent and when to be our friend. She didn't take the easy route of being friends with us when we were kids—she focused on raising us to be strong and resilient. I'm so thankful for that."

Likability and her constant efforts at self-improvement were two of Angie's personality traits that stand out to Margaret. "She was a go-getter. It was always go, go, go with her. She was a curious and intuitive person who always was looking for a project or to challenge herself with something new." An example Margaret cited was when Angie decided she wanted to get certified as a personal trainer. She did the training on time and achieved the certification.

Margaret says it was all thanks to Angie that the Weber home felt so warm and welcoming. "We loved being together, no matter what we were doing. The house was always full of laughter, and it had such a friendly atmosphere that our friends couldn't help but want to be there. We always had people over, just hanging out and staying for dinner."

Regarding Angie's drive to improve herself, Margaret said the best example is her decision to pursue a nursing career in her early forties. She worked hard to earn her RN, BS and master's degrees in nursing. "She set a great example for us to choose our goals and do our best to achieve them."

After Margaret graduated from the University of Nebraska, she lived with her folks in Wisconsin for the summer until she landed her first job. "Our relationship at that time evolved into a friendship. Mom always showed her love and affection, but we were adult friends, too." Margaret recalls a surprise fiftieth birthday party hosted by me when Angie said to her and sister Kathleen, "I just love my girls."

When Angie was diagnosed with terminal brain cancer, Margaret remembers that she didn't complain or feel sorry for herself. "She never said she was scared about her future and didn't put an emotional load on us." When Angie phoned her children with the news of her diagnosis, she called Margaret last. "Mom knew I was the most emotional of the kids and I would outwardly take it the hardest." Given the cancer history in the O'Donnell family (six of eight family members had cancer and four died from it), Margaret wonders if Angie thought she wouldn't live a long life and wanted to cram as much activity and achievement as possible. Maybe that was the source of her go, go, go mindset.

Margaret says she takes after her mother's let's-do-it attitude. "Like Mom, I'd rather ask for forgiveness than ask for permission."

Michael

Youngest child Michael is thirty-one, married with a baby daughter, Blair. He married Maura in 2021. They live in Shaker Heights, Ohio. He works at home for a consulting group that specializes in finance management for healthcare organizations.

Michael is also the only Weber child who had a business relationship with his mother. "I was always asking Mom for money and she made a deal with me. For twenty-five dollars every two months, I would make coffee in the morning before she left for work and I would defrost a chicken or other food she wanted to cook for dinner. It was a nice arrangement for me but she could have bought her coffee every morning at McDonald's for a buck," Michael said.

Being the youngest, Michael recalls having more freedom than his siblings did when in high school. "I had a longer leash but she kept me accountable," he said. Michael describes his mother as caring, very personable, quick-witted, and street smart. "She didn't take herself too seriously and had a spontaneous sense of humor. It came naturally. She didn't try to be funny."

Angie was quick to defend her children and did so with Michael when she battled with his third- grade teacher over what she perceived to be unfair treatment of her son. In a confrontation, Angie was livid and expressed her disgust with the teacher.

Michael recalls that Angie had a unique way of showing her displeasure when the children were careless. He left his clothes in the dryer too long one day when Angie had a load she wanted to put in the dryer. So, she took out Mike's clothes and threw them outside. Another time, when Michael left a dirty dish in the sink, Angie put the dish on his bed. Message sent.

Michael concurs with his siblings in appreciating how Angie fostered a culture of closeness in the family. "She always kept it light and balanced. For example, on our last Costa Rica trip she was fun and carefree despite being sick. There was never any doom and gloom from her about the cancer, and she always would carve out time to do things with us."

Girlfriends: Colleen and Marion and Our Neighbor Lauren

Marion introduced Angie and me. They had become best friends while in high school dating back to their time working the switchboard at the Martinique/Drury Lane Theater. Angie first knew Colleen as the wife of one of her oldest brother's good friends. After we were married, we socialized often and took trips with Colleen and her husband Dan.

Marion describes Angie as always being positive and determined. "She would set her sights on a goal and achieve it. She always wanted to get to the next level." When Marion was hired as a sales representative for Victor Technologies, she learned there was an opening for an executive secretary and recommended Angie. She got the job, and that started her business career.

"Angie was always optimistic about everything she could achieve and for the future," Colleen recalls. "She was steadily driven to be an improved or better version of herself, be it professional or personal."

"As friends we were good for each other," said Marion. "She was my only female friend who understood the challenges of being a woman in the corporate world. We shared so much together."

For fifteen years, Marion and Angie shopped on Black Friday starting at 5:00 a.m. They would hit Venture first to get gifts for our kids and they were done by 9:00. Angie hauled out several bags of presents. Their next stop was the mall. "That's when we shopped for ourselves," Marion said. "We were always looking for bargains."

"When we were staying at the Webers' Wisconsin home, I noticed that Angie complimented her kids on something they did, saying, 'Good job,'" said Colleen. "It made me think how often I did not do the same for our kids and it encouraged me to do more of that."

Every spring, Angie and Marion would spend a work weekend at the lake house to do extensive cleaning and get the place in shape for the summer. "We worked our tails off and finished cleaning in the late afternoon. We rewarded ourselves by drinking two bottles of chardonnay," Marion said.

"She was so brave and caring. She worried about you, Chuck. She worried who was going to take care of you when she was gone. She worried about me, too," Marion noted. Marion was with us at Northwestern Memorial Hospital for Angie's first brain surgery. She recalls that Angie told her over lunch two days before the operation that she was scared about the bad headaches and sleeping so much. After the operation, we converged in Angie's hospital room and it was supposed to be family only. Angie insisted that the nurses allow Marion in the room.

Throughout our brain cancer ordeal, I called Colleen an angel of mercy because she would visit an impaired and dying Angie every week. She drove two hours each way to see her. "It's what a friend would do," Colleen insisted. "I wanted you and Angie to know you are not alone."

"I remember when she lost her hair. She had great spirit about it and said, 'Now we look alike,' meaning you and her," Marion remembered. "I always called her my little Irish flower blossom. Once I asked her on Saint Patrick's Day where her green was. She told me she didn't need to wear green to prove she was Irish."

Lauren was a year older than Kathleen and at the time was her best friend. She lived next door to us in Palatine and was a frequent weekend visitor at the lake.

"Angie Weber was like a second mom to me. I think about her every day and wish that my memories of her were stronger and more vivid." Lauren recalled Angie cleaning the lake house with Whitney Houston blasting and helping her off a soccer field when she sprained an ankle.

"Without ever giving it a second thought, she allowed me to be part of her family. She challenged me like my own mother did, from making me lock my seat belt in the minivan, to cleaning the toilets before leaving Whitewater, to teaching me that blow-drying my hair upside down would give it more volume. She had the best laugh, loved so passionately, and kept going when things were probably hard."

The Sisters: Mimi and Kathleen

Mimi is Angie's older sister and a retired cardiac-care nurse. She married Gene in 1984 and has five children and twelve grandchildren. Kathleen, our oldest daughter's namesake, is a podiatrist. She married John in 1989 and has four children, all men. At her wedding, Kathleen recalls that Angie "was huge expecting Charlie."

Mimi and Angie talked on the phone almost every day. Even today an impulse will come to her while driving that she has to call Angie. "I miss her so much and think about her every day. She would do anything for you and was a lot of fun to be with," she said. Mimi and Angie shared an apartment in the Marquette Park neighborhood for four years until Mimi got married. "She was never crabby and was very quick-witted."

Kathleen offers memories about Angie from her perspective as the youngest child in the family and being five years younger than Angie. "I looked up to her. She was very cool to me, and we always had a good time together." She remembers being with Angie for a full night of partying in a local bar and then going bowling at 4:00 a.m. when the bar closed. "Angie was a partier and later on asked me not to tell her kids about how she sowed her wild oats."

Angie, Mimi, and Kathleen often danced in the kitchen of their parents' house. Today, Kathleen plays the radio in her podiatry office and two songs triggered that memory. She heard Bette Midler singing "Boogie Woogie Bugle Boy" and Bill Haley's "Rock Around the Clock" one day on the radio, and they reminded her of those kitchen dance parties.

Mimi recalls when Angie decided to pursue a master's degree in nursing and convinced her to join her in the effort. "After decades working in nursing, I didn't want or need a master's degree, but Angie was persistent and convinced me to enroll in the program. I'm glad she talked me into it because it was an enjoyable experience, and Angie got straight A's."

Kathleen remembers that Angie loved animals. "She had hamsters and guinea pigs, and when a pizza we ordered arrived, a cat jumped into the house and Angie kept it."

Angie's siblings and their friends in early February would head to the Upper Peninsula of Michigan for a ski weekend. She was a good skier and more than kept up her end of the partying in the rented chalet. In 2016, the last time Angie went on that trip, the group went snowmobiling instead of skiing. Angie piloted her own snowmobile but had to stop midway on the trail because she was tired. Back in their chalet that night, Angie brought tears to her siblings' eyes when she said: "I know what's going to happen to me."

There were two road trips Angie organized for her sisters and their children in 2003 and 2004. The first road trip destination was to Destin, Florida. Angie did all the driving in our Chevy Suburban. "There were seven of us and we had a penthouse apartment on the gulf in Destin. The kids had a great time splashing in the gulf," Mimi remembers. She added that a week after they left Destin, the town was ravaged by a hurricane. The second road trip took Angie, the two sisters, and eleven children to Asheville, North Carolina. There they visited the famed Biltmore Estate built by the Vanderbilt family. Angie was very impressed by the huge wine cellar.

At a McDonald's in North Carolina, a guy looked at the crew and said, "Are they all of your kids?" Angie said yes and later told Kathleen she didn't want to say that two were left at home.

Kathleen noted that Angie had a good heart and was an exceptional mother. "She was firm but gave her kids a long leash and wanted them to follow their own paths. She was not overbearing and provided a stable home life. Her mantra was 'Let them.'" She remembered Angie showing empathy with our daughter Margaret who sometimes struggled to get good grades in high school, and that she was very excited for our daughter Kathleen when she was accepted at Marquette University. "Angie's kids are a credit to her," Kathleen said.

When Mimi and Kathleen learned the news of Angie's cancer diagnosis, their sister tried to comfort them by not getting emotional and assuring them that she would be okay. She even joked about some upcoming dental work which was supposed to last for 10 or more years. She said the dental work didn't need to last very long. When she spotted a woman in a wheelchair, Angie said, "I hope I don't get like that."

"She was very brave and I never saw her break down, even though she knew there wasn't much time left for her," Mimi said. Kathleen added that on a phone call with Angie before her third surgery on January 31, 2017, her sister said, "Don't cry. I'll be fine."

Work Colleagues: Michelle and Peg

Michelle was Angie's best friend at Oracle and remembers that Angie was highly regarded at the company for her intelligence, efficiency at getting onerous paperwork done, and ability to work with aggressive sales people who often had last-minute demands. "She was very personable, open and easygoing, able to work well with others, and always willing to share her knowledge," she said. "Angie also could tell it like it is when she had to, but in positive ways without harshness. When I started at Oracle in 1997, it was Angie who made me feel welcome and befriended me." Michelle is now a vice president and has worked at Oracle for thirty-seven years.

Angie and I enjoyed dinners with Michelle and her husband Paul through the years at different restaurants in the northwest suburbs. Like us, Michelle and Paul were wine lovers. One of our favorite outings was a pre-Christmas lunch at an expensive and popular French restaurant in Arlington Heights. Lunch began at 1:00 p.m.

with champagne and ended late in the afternoon with cognac or port. It was a great way to kick off the holiday season.

During Angie's tenure at Baxter, Peg was her closest occupational health nurse colleague. Peg is retired from Baxter.

"At work, Angie always was upbeat, funny, and pragmatic. She was great to hang with," Peg remembers. She added that Angie was known as a hard worker who did her share and more, especially when the company nurses had to give flu shots to employees at Baxter's Round Lake, Illinois corporate campus.

Every year, Peg and Angie would travel to attend the American Association of Occupational Health Nurses conference. They would attend educational sessions in the morning and then enjoy wine poolside in the afternoons. One day they broke four corkscrews trying to open a stubborn bottle of wine.

Angie was a guiding force behind the construction of a new employee fitness center at Round Lake. Peg recalls Angie worked out there every day. "She was so fit and athletic." In late summer in 2013, Peg was the first in the company who noticed that Angie's cognitive ability was slipping. "She sent an email that was basically incoherent, and everyone who received it knew she was off and not herself."

I called Peg to inform her about the brain cancer diagnosis and Angie's first surgery. After her sick leave had lapsed, Angie returned to work and Peg said she was fully capable of resuming her duties. "She was amazing after the first surgery. We had an occupational health department bowling outing soon after she returned to work, and Angie took first place with a 200 game." Her colleagues autographed a bowling pin for her to commemorate the achievement. The pin sits on a bookshelf in the lake house.

Peg said there was a noticeable decline in Angie's performance after the second surgery. There were some record-keeping problems she was blamed for but Angie angrily defended herself. Her manager, however, believed Angie's medical issues posed a risk to employee health and safety if she continued in her nursing job. She was laid off and her Baxter career was over.

Today, Peg fondly remembers a cheerful colleague and her achievements as a certified occupational health nurse.

Conclusion

WHY ANGIE MATTERS

> "Death leaves a heartache no one can heal, love
> leaves a memory no one can steal."
>
> — From a sympathy card

The kids arrived at the house in the afternoon and we discussed funeral arrangements. I phoned the assistant funeral director at Davenport Funeral Home, and she checked available times for Angie's wake and funeral. The wake would be held on Friday, January 12, and the funeral Mass would be on Saturday morning, January 13. The next day, all of us headed to Illinois to meet with the assistant funeral director and a staff member at St. Theresa. At the funeral home, per Angie's wishes, we opted for cremation and picked out an urn for the ashes, which would be buried at Mount Olivet Catholic Cemetery in Janesville. We were asked if we wanted Angie's ashes processed into earrings. We unanimously said no. Next, she asked if any of any of us wanted to keep a lock of Angie's hair. I said yes but no one else wanted hair. I was surprised.

At St. Theresa Church we planned the funeral Mass, picked the Scripture verses, selected the readers, and chose the hymns. We rejected the suggested recessional hymn, which was "On Eagles' Wings." I said, "It's too sad. We sang it at my mother's funeral in 1987 and I bawled my eyes out." Instead, we chose "How Great Thou Art."

More than five hundred mourners attended the wake and funeral. From 6:30 to 8:30 p.m., the wake was crowded and noisy. A television monitor showed years of memories in a continuous loop photo array. The wake and funeral were wonderful tributes to Angie. I was overwhelmed with the outpouring of love for her and of the support extended to our family. One of the mourners at the wake comforted me with something Angie said to him. He was a member of Angie's running club and mentioned that Angie told him that my love and support gave her the personal and professional confidence she needed. I choked up when I heard that.

Angie left a proud and beautiful legacy. I see her in the mannerisms and personal traits shown by our four children. All have inherited Angie's passionate zeal for self-improvement, her compassion for others, and her wonderful sense of humor. The girls have her boisterous laugh.

So let's ask: Why does Angie matter? I believe Angie is an inspiration for those who might believe the odds in life are stacked against them. Angie's life is the inspiring story of a woman who faced obstacles throughout her life and summoned all her ambitions and limitless energy to overcome them and achieve personal and professional success.

She overcame an early obstacle thrown in her path by indifferent parents who couldn't provide the strong support and encouragement she needed. She did not let her lack of a college degree stop her from succeeding at Oracle. She confronted the obstacle of advancing age to embark on a major career change into nursing in her forties and worked hard to obtain the educational credentials she needed for her new career. On the personal side, she overcame obstacles confronting working moms and she deftly balanced her roles at work and at home. She never was too busy to help and care for her children. The kids have said she set a powerful example of love, ambition, and determination for them that has guided their lives.

Angie was a physical fitness enthusiast, worked out daily, and accepted the challenge of running marathon races in her forties. She completed eleven marathons.

Finally, she boldly confronted what turned out to be an insurmountable obstacle—cancer. When she was first diagnosed in 2013, she confronted the obstacle to her health and life posed by glioblastoma. She endured chemotherapy, radiation, and hair loss without complaining or feeling sorry for herself. After completing her first round of treatment, she overcame possible limitations that might have prevented her from returning to work. She came back and colleagues said she was as good as new. When the cancer returned just five months later, she was determined to combat this setback, and once again she recovered and returned to work. She didn't let a would-be deadly cancer stop her from living her life to the fullest. Our family was inspired by Angie's courage and zest for life. Her example helped us cope with her disease. She did not feel sorry for herself. The only time I heard her complain is when she hugged me one morning while we were getting dressed and said, "I'm going to miss everything."

The last obstacle Angie faced was the coma that felled her after the third surgery. We saw her lie helpless in the ICU unit, but I knew she was fighting for her life even though we saw no overt evidence. The doctors were not sure she would wake up. However, she awakened from the coma and overcame the recovery obstacle by succeeding with physical rehab for several months and regaining her ability to move and speak. Her fight was over when the white matter in her brain became irreparably damaged from radiation treatments given four years earlier.

Why does Angie matter? She matters because hope matters. Her lifelong journey battling and overcoming obstacles can and should inspire anyone struggling with self-doubt, fearing what the future might hold, lacking confidence to set goals and achieve them, being hesitant to seize control of one's life, and failing to learn how to enjoy life in good times and bad. Angie is an authentic source of inspiration and hope.

Angie still inspires me. Every day, I cherish memories of our life together. I talk to her. She always will be the love of my life. Angie is my hero.

The Communication Department at the University of Wisconsin-Whitewater offers a major in corporate and health communication. Angie was a devoted employee health communicator in her role as an occupational health nurse. This year, 2025, I am funding a partial scholarship in Angie's honor for students in that program.

> "Though you say goodbye for now, it is only until you meet again someday—when your emptiness will turn to fulfillment, your despair to joy, and you will love again for eternity in that place where no one grows old."
>
> —Verse from a sympathy card

ACKNOWLEDGEMENTS

My heartfelt thanks to those who shared their thoughts and memories about Angie during our interviews.

Kathleen Frost

Charlie Weber

Margaret Weber

Michael Weber

Mary Diamond

Kathleen Daly

Marion Gentile

Colleen Liberacki

Michelle Myer

Peg Gorman

ABOUT THE AUTHOR

Chuck Weber resides in Whitewater, Wisconsin and is a retired public relations consultant. He now teaches at the University of Wisconsin-Whitewater. He was married to Angela Weber for thirty-three years and cherishes her memory in this memoir. He has four adult children and seven grandchildren.